CULTURE
SHIFT

CULTURE SHIFT

Transforming Your Church from the Inside Out

Foreword by Erwin Raphael McManus

Robert Lewis, Wayne Cordeiro

with Warren Bird

A LEADERSHIP NETWORK PUBLICATION

JOSSEY-BASS
A Wiley Imprint
www.josseybass.com

Published by Jossey-Bass
A Wiley Imprint
989 Market Street, San Francisco, CA 94103-1741   www.josseybass.com

Jossey-Bass books and products are available through most bookstores. To contact Jossey-Bass directly call our Customer Care Department within the U.S. at 800-956-7739, outside the U.S. at 317-572-3986, or fax 317-572-4002.

Jossey-Bass also publishes its books in a variety of electronic formats. Some content that appears in print may not be available in electronic books.

Unless otherwise noted, Scripture quotations taken from the New American Standard Bible®, Copyright © 1960, 1962, 1963, 1968, 1971, 1972, 1973, 1975, 1977, 1995 by The Lockman Foundation. Used by permission. (www.Lockman.org)

Other translations used: The Message: The Bible in Contemporary Language, GNT (Good News Translation), KJV (King James Version), NKJV (New King James Version), NLT (New Living Translation), NRSV (New Revised Standard Version)and Phillips (The New Testament in Modern English translated by J. B. Phillips)

Library of Congress Cataloging-in-Publication Data

Lewis, Robert, date.
  Culture shift: transforming your church from the inside out / Robert Lewis, Wayne Cordeiro, with Warren Bird; foreword by Erwin Raphael McManus.—1st ed.
       p. cm.
Includes bibliographical references and index.
      ISBN 0-7879-7530-3 (alk. paper)
   1. Church renewal. 2. Christianity and culture. I. Cordeiro, Wayne. II. Bird, Warren. III. Title.
   BV600.3.L49 2005
   253—dc22

                                                          2004027928

Printed in the United States of America
FIRST EDITION
HB Printing   10 9 8 7 6 5 4 3 2 1

LEADERSHIP NETWORK TITLES

Leading from the Second Chair: Serving Your Church, Fulfilling Your Role, and Realizing Your Dreams, by Mike Bonem and Roger Patterson

The Way of Jesus: A Journey of Freedom for Pilgrims and Wanderers, by Jonathan Campbell with Jennifer Campbell

Leading the Team-Based Church: How Pastors and Church Staffs Can Grow Together into a Powerful Fellowship of Leaders, by George Cladis

Leading Congregational Change Workbook, by James H. Furr, Mike Bonem, and Jim Herrington

Leading Congregational Change: A Practical Guide for the Transformational Journey, by Jim Herrington, Mike Bonem, and James H. Furr

The Leader's Journey: Accepting the Call to Personal and Congregational Transformation, by Jim Herrington, Robert Creech, and Trisha Taylor

Culture Shift: Transforming Your Church from the Inside Out, by Robert Lewis, Wayne Cordeiro, with Warren Bird

A New Kind of Christian: A Tale of Two Friends on a Spiritual Journey, by Brian McLaren

The Story We Find Ourselves in: Further Adventures of a New Kind of Christian, by Brian McLaren

The Present Future: Six Tough Questions for the Church, by Reggie McNeal

A Work of Heart: Understanding How God Shapes Spiritual Leaders, by Reggie McNeal

The Millennium Matrix: Reclaiming the Past, Reframing the Future of the Church, by M. Rex Miller

Shaped by God's Heart: The Passion and Practices of Missional Churches, by Milfred Minatrea

The Ascent of a Leader: How Ordinary Relationships Develop Extraordinary Character and Influence, by Bill Thrall, Bruce McNicol, and Ken McElrath

The Elephant in the Boardroom: Speaking the Unspoken About Pastoral Transition, by Carolyn Weese and J. Russell Crabtree

Contents

About Leadership Network

Since 1984, Leadership Network has fostered church innovation and growth by diligently pursuing its far-reaching mission statement: *To identify, connect and help high-capacity Christian leaders multiply their impact.*

While Leadership Network's techniques adapt and change as the Church faces new opportunities and challenges, the organization's work follows a consistent and proven pattern:

Leadership Network brings together entrepreneurial leaders who are focused on similar ministry initiatives. The ensuing collaboration—often across denominational lines—provides a strong base from which individual leaders can better analyze and refine their individual strategies. Peer-to-peer interaction, dialogue and sharing inevitably accelerate participants' own innovations and ideas. Leadership Network further enhances this process through the development and distribution of highly targeted ministry tools and resources—including audio and video programs, special reports, e-publications and online downloads.

With Leadership Network's assistance, today's Christian leaders are energized, equipped, inspired—and better able to multiply their own dynamic Kingdom-building initiatives.

Launched in 1996 in conjunction with Jossey-Bass, a Wiley Imprint, *Leadership Network Publications* present *thoroughly researched and innovative concepts* from leading thinkers, practitioners, and pioneering churches. The series collectively draws from a wide range of disciplines with individual titles providing perspective on one or more of five primary areas:

- Enabling effective leadership
- Encouraging life-changing service
- Building authentic community
- Creating kingdom-centered impact
- Engaging cultural and demographic realities

For additional information on the mission or activities of Leadership Network activities, please contact:

Leadership Network
2501 Cedar Springs, Suite 200
Dallas, Texas 75201
800.765.5323
client.care@leadnet.org

Foreword

by Erwin Raphael McManus

Culture Shift is about regaining the power of an apostolic ethos. Jesus Christ began a revolution that transformed individuals and created a transformational community. Everything recorded in the book of Acts is the outcome and overflow of this apostolic ethos. Ethos—the fuel of movements—is the tribal fire of a culture.

Acts 4:32 paints a picture of many hearts bound together. It says, "All the believers were one in heart and mind." Their environment fused a belief in the awesome nature of God with a stewardship of each person's God-given potential. These elements were at the same time powerfully unifying and contagiously expanding.

The challenge that many congregations face, which *Culture Shift* addresses, is how to build a culture that's irresistible. I had the privilege of being part of the early conversations that led to the development of this book. The original idea was to put together the best practices of churches that are skilled at improvisation. In a strange kind of way, great leaders don't always know where they are going, but they always get you where you need to go. You can show improvisational leaders where the starting blocks are, and you can tell them where the finish line is, but how they get there is a part of their own genius.

Long-term pastors Robert Lewis and Wayne Cordeiro share the rare gift of being able to teach others how to improvise. They show you how to think but not what to think. They focus on the creation of an improvisational ethos rather than on the skill of improvisation.

When I think of Robert Lewis and Wayne Cordeiro, what immediately comes to mind are strong leaders who are highly disciplined and extremely focused. Though one is in Arkansas and the other in Hawaii, they have much in common. Both of their ministries are known for relevance, innovation, adaptability, and results. They both have a whatever-it-takes mentality. Yet in the end it is their ability to unleash the gifts, talents, passions, and energy of all who join them that sets them apart. It is important for them to write on this subject, not because they themselves are masters of improvisation but because they have nurtured a culture in which the church is no longer reactive but proactive; no longer institutional but improvisational.

When I wrote *An Unstoppable Force,*[1] conversations about church growth were dominated by models, systems, and processes—all of which are important. It felt like I was spitting into the wind, but I was determined to at least move us to change the focus of our conversation from methods to essence. Becoming a first-century church in this third millennium cannot be about rediscovering or reestablishing ancient praxis, however refreshing it may feel in contrast to modern expressions of faith. What must be rediscovered is the essence of an apostolic ethos. This ethos is borne out of a movement that could be described as nothing less than improvisational. Yet "when we awaken the apostolic ethos, the heart of God begins to pulsate throughout the church of Jesus Christ."[2]

Ironically, if you break down everything I have ever put into print, it is at its core calling us to a life of shaping culture through improvisation. How can you possibly live a life that is responsive to the Spirit of God if you lack this essential competency? If in the past a church could exist without a Spirit-pliable culture, it is certainly not true in the present and will be even less possible in the future.

Can your church create and shape culture? I am convinced that not only is the answer yes, but more than anything else, this is what the church must do. Too often when we claim we are waiting on God, he is waiting on us.

Culture Shift may not give you all the answers you want or even need, but it will place you in the conversation and point you in the direction that will be the difference between ministry paralysis and a community of faith that powerfully and creatively advances the kingdom of God.

Unleashing the Spirit of Creativity,

Erwin Raphael McManus
Lead Pastor and Cultural Architect, Mosaic, Los Angeles
www.mosaic.org

*This book is dedicated to all those who tried and failed
but who have the heart and willingness to try again.*

*You are still pursuing God's best, and you refuse to give up
until your church becomes more like the kingdom of God.
May God give you the courage you need to get there.*

Preface

Culture Shift, born out of a passion we both hold deeply, is written to help you develop an irresistible culture in your congregation. The idea of church culture is often ignored, in part because so little material is available about it. Yet we believe *culture is to the church what a soul is to the human body*. It is an overall life force that the Holy Spirit uses to give energy, personality, and uniqueness to everything a body of believers says and does.

As two pastors long in the trenches of everyday church life, we are absolutely convinced of the primacy of giving attention to church culture. It influences everything you do. It colors the way you choose and introduce programs. It shapes how you select and train leaders.

Indeed, each time we met to work on this book, again and again we found ourselves passionate about bringing this critical but often overlooked issue into the focus and reach of all types of churches—long-established and new, small and large, homogenous and multiracial. We hope to help pastors and church leaders like yourself look *within* to your culture before looking *without* to Band-Aid solutions and hastily grabbed programs. Quick fixes may inject a momentary spiritual high, but can never deliver the more radical, transformational power you hope for.

Transformation can never be brought in from the outside. Transformation is inside work, and believe it or not, you already possess the elements that can bring it about. Through God's design, everything you need is right there in your midst!

> Transformation can never be brought in from the outside. Through God's design, everything you need is right there in your midst!

A rich culture, we believe, is the hidden treasure most church leaders are really looking for when they travel outside to workshops and conferences in search of transformational answers. But it's not based in an out-of-state event. It's back home where you live. And our desire is to help you tap into it and unleash it.

Part One begins our journey by bringing this matter of culture into clear view. The concepts and stories we present there will help you embrace the priority of culture and understand how it is the first cause behind so much of what a church is or hopes to become.

Part Two becomes more practical. The first key question it helps you answer is, What is the distinctive culture of this church?—referring to the local group of believers you love, serve, and partner with in mission for God. How do you get a handle on your church's culture? The answer will require more than reading on your part. The practical applications in these chapters are meant to help you personalize this information. We hope that they will result in a hands-on, unambiguous identification of the culture now within your church.

This then leads to a second important question: How do you change a church culture? Again, we offer practical steps to shift the culture of your church to new life. As you will discover, this process is much different from the patchwork approaches so often called on from the outside to fix the problem. A culture-focused approach is much more radical, with an altogether different emphasis. But it is one that truly transforms—which is what many pastors and church leaders are deeply hungering for today.

In Parts Three and Four, we present an insider's look at our two churches. New Hope Christian Fellowship O'ahu (where Wayne Cordeiro serves) and Fellowship Bible Church (where Robert Lewis serves) are vastly different churches above ground. You will quickly see and experience those differences as you read each of our stories in these sections called "Growing the Culture" and "Advancing the Culture." And yet, below ground, we are very much alike. We both make it our first priority to protect, cultivate, and enrich the cultures of our churches.

Indeed, every vibrant church has learned to partner with the Holy Spirit in developing a thriving, contagious, irresistible culture, as Part Five affirms. A healthy culture is crucial to such churches' success and power. Vastly different expressions of ministry may flow out of them or their fruit may come in varied colors and sizes, but they are all healthy cultures first! And they instinctively or intentionally know how to stay healthy as well.

From start to finish, *Culture Shift* helps you advance the right culture. You'll learn how to recognize signs of forward progress. You'll smell what it looks like when you're getting there. You'll be encouraged to keep pressing forward.

Culture first. This is what we want every church leader to know, understand, appreciate, applaud, and then cultivate. That's because real transformation only flows one way: from the inside out!

Robert Lewis
Little Rock, Arkansas

Wayne Cordeiro
Honolulu, Hawaii

CULTURE
SHIFT

Awakening to Culture

DAVID LIVINGSTONE WAS EAGER TO TRAVEL into the uncharted lands of Central Africa to preach the gospel. On one occasion, the famous nineteenth-century missionary and explorer arrived at the edge of a large territory that was ruled by a tribal chieftain. According to tradition, the chief would come out to meet him there; Livingstone could go forward only after an exchange was made. The chief would choose any item of Livingstone's personal property that caught his fancy and keep it for himself, while giving the missionary something of his own in return.

Livingstone had few possessions with him, but at their encounter he obediently spread them all out on the ground—his clothes, his books, his watch, and even the goat that provided him with milk (since chronic stomach problems kept him from drinking the local water). To his dismay, the chief took the goat. In return, the chief gave him a carved stick, shaped like a walking cane.

Livingstone was most disappointed. He began to gripe to God about what he viewed as a stupid walking cane. What could it do for him, compared to the goat who kept him well?

Then one of the local men explained, "That's not a walking cane. It's the king's very own scepter, and with it you will find entrance to every village in our country. The king has honored you greatly."

The man was right. God opened Central Africa to Livingstone, and as successive evangelists followed him wave after wave of conversions occurred.

* * * * *

We believe that when you find the keys to the culture of your own church, it will give you the power of the king's scepter. New doors will open to you. Dreams you've had for transforming, revitalizing, or strengthening your church will now have a way to become reality.

Church culture is foundational to the life and witness of every church. Unfortunately, too many church leaders fail to recognize or understand the implications of this reality. Others grasp the concept but want practical guidance about the culture of the church they serve: how to identify it, how to change it, and how to keep it aligned with their church's mission.

This first part of *Culture Shift* prepares you to do just that. It is designed to help you, as a leader in your church, awaken to the unique culture represented by the church—both what it is and what it can be.

Why Culture Matters

CULTURE IS THE MOST IMPORTANT SOCIAL REALITY IN your church. Though invisible to the untrained eye, its power is undeniable. Culture gives color and flavor to everything your church is and does. Like a powerful current running through your church, it can move you inland or take you farther out to sea. It can prevent your church's potential from ever being realized, or—if used by the Holy Spirit—it can draw others in and reproduce healthy spiritual life all along the way.

Culture is also an enigma. It defies simple definition and is difficult to explain. It's not a "plug and play" program that you buy off the shelf. Nor is it something you can clone from another church that seems successful.

You might underestimate its capacity for helping you or blocking you, just as you probably don't think regularly about the role of the air you breathe. Yet to make any kind of transition as a church, *your church's culture can't be ignored.* Only if you play an active role in shifting the culture can you best help your church to become the organic, life-giving environment you've always known it can be.

Here is a story to start you on a journey of awakening to the importance of the culture in your church.

"Travis doesn't want to go back home," Nate said as the three other church leaders sat down with him for lunch. The occasion was a church conference promising the latest ideas for ministry. For now, though, they were enjoying the opportunity to catch up with each other.

"What's up?" Dan, the senior pastor, probed.

"Travis is that fifteen-year-old in the detention home for high-risk kids. One of our youth teams has been working with him," Nate explained.

The others were aware of the situation.

"He's attended all the classes and is now convinced that drugs will ruin him," Nate continued. "Best of all, he opened his heart to Christ! On graduation day, Luis and I were there to celebrate with him."

Luis, who was relatively new to the church and was in training to be a volunteer youth sponsor, explained what happened next. "After the ceremony, Travis looked at me very seriously and said, 'I don't want to go home.'"

"Why in the world doesn't he want to go home?" asked Brianna, a church staff member. "Isn't that what he's been working toward for the last six months?"

"What Travis told me next shocked me," Nate replied. "He told us, 'If you send me home, I'll run away as soon as I arrive. You see, it was my parents who introduced me to this stuff in the first place. If I go back home, I'll fall back in to the habit that I've just spent the last six months trying to kick!'"

Dan, with twenty years of ministry under his belt nodded knowingly. "He's going back a different person, but everyone there is still the same. The odds are stacked against him."

There was a pause in the conversation. Everyone at the table knew the challenges Travis would face at home.

"I feel that way sometimes," said Brianna, sounding a little on edge. Dan sensed that the conversation was shifting from Travis to church matters.

"You don't want to go home either, after this conference?" he asked with a concerned smile.

The others looked at Brianna, sensing a bit of tension.

"It's not that," Brianna quickly replied. "But when we go back to church, and we're all filled with great ideas from a conference like this one, it's frustrating. It's like pushing water uphill."

The rest of them felt the tension building and waited with apprehension for her to continue.

"It's like with Travis," she said, trying to explain. "*He* has changed, but he's going home to a place that refuses to change. It's one person pushing against an environment that seems to oppose everything he's learned."

Dan's expression suggested he didn't seem to catch the significance of what she was saying.

"It's the culture!" she blurted. "You know, like when people talk about corporate culture—the unspoken message about 'the way we do things here.' The culture hasn't changed in his home. And when people like us come back from conferences like this one, great ideas go nowhere if the culture is unreceptive."

> Great ideas go nowhere if the culture is unreceptive.

Dan, Nate, and Luis looked awkwardly at each other, and then at Brianna.

After a few seconds of awkward silence, she added, "Seems like as leaders it's our job to transform the culture at our own church so that healthy ideas have fertile soil to take root in and grow."

Dan started to respond but then paused. He didn't really know what to say.

"Looks like they're calling us back to the next session," Nate said, trying to ease the tension.

As they walked back to the session, Dan finally said, "If the snag is the culture at our church, how can we change it? It seems like an overwhelming task to me. Where do you start?"

"Maybe one of the speakers will talk about that issue," said Luis hopefully.

"Culture isn't a subject that a conference like this one will speak to," said Brianna. This was a subject she'd been thinking about. "It's a more organic issue."

No one responded, because they were already tuned into the conference, looking for that next great idea.

COULD THIS BE YOUR CHURCH?

Dan, Luis, Nate, and Brianna made a good start on understanding the problem, but they couldn't find the help they needed to take the next step. Still, some churches *do* discover how to build the right culture from the inside out. When that happens, their community takes notice. Stories emerge about forgiveness, reconciliation, hope, love, joy, help in adversity, and power for daily living. People living in the area around this particular church, no matter what their faith background, identify it as a community representing the hands and arms of God.

Churches like this one really do exist! They may vary in size and represent many denominations and worship styles, but they all have one quality in common: they "do church" from the inside out. Instead of looking outside for the next great program that will change them, they begin making changes with themselves. As each church births a healthy God-honoring culture, community people come out of the woodwork to experience it.

Healthy churches "do church" from the inside out.

What about *your* church? Would you like it to be an island of health that magnetically draws people who feel lost, seasick, or shipwrecked? Or people who are simply in need of solid ground on which to build their lives?

Your church can indeed make certain changes and *become the way church was always meant to be.* Such changes focus not so much on the latest new idea or program but on a culture shift that honors your church's unique values. How do we know? Because each of us (Robert Lewis and Wayne Cordeiro) has experienced this in our own quite different churches.

Our churches are worlds apart—Robert's is in Arkansas and Wayne's is in Hawaii—but we're on remarkably parallel pathways. God has birthed an authentic, life-giving culture at each church, and it has drawn people one by one, then by tens, and now by hundreds and thousands each year. More important, the people who come are finding the kind of help they seek. They're getting better, finding Christ, and maturing in every way.

Our approach is not a quick fix. It avoids a plug-and-play, one-size-fits-all program. Instead it's a *culture shift:* a new different way of thinking about church, one that works in Arkansas and Hawaii, and in all other geographies and circumstances.

How can we make such an assertive claim? God's Word offers it, and the power of the Holy Spirit is doing it in many places. This culture shift can come to your town, beginning with your church. We believe it's your birthright, your spiritual inheritance, something promised to you by God.

IDENTIFYING YOUR INHERITANCE

Imagine a billionaire's child who was promised money as a birthright. Or better, imagine *you* are the heir. You're eight years old and you have a multibillionaire dad who intends to give you his estate as an inheritance. You are to receive it at age twenty-one.

Your loving father hires someone to tutor you so that when you turn twenty-one you will have the depth, character, and wisdom necessary to steward all that money. Your tutor has a degree of authority but doesn't dictate your life. Instead, the tutor creates a nurturing yet challenging culture to assist you in growing toward an appropriate level of skill and stature. The tutor serves you, helping you come into your inheritance as a delight to your father.

Sound far-fetched? That's exactly what happened in ancient Greek society. Paul describes such a situation in Galatians 4:1–2: "As long as the heir is a child, he does not differ at all from a slave although he is owner of everything, but he is under guardians and managers until the date set by the father."

No matter how wealthy the father may be, the child cannot yet enjoy the wealth. The money belongs to the child but cannot be possessed and used by the child until he or she reaches the age stipulated in the trust.

The tutor's job is to build an appropriate culture so a youth will be ready for an inheritance. By analogy, church leaders are the primary tutors God uses to lead believers personally and practically into a rich experience of the salvation that is theirs. The spiritual wealth is already there, set aside and waiting to be inherited. But this wealthy potential can be released congregationally only if the right tutors produce the right culture for receiving it. That's the job of *church leadership*.

Are you in love with the potential that's in your church? Do you see the great potential God has already willed to it? As a leader, you're the tutor God has called to release it.

YES, YOUR CHURCH

Your church, whatever its size or age, has billion-dollar potential. Yes, your church, and every church where the Spirit of God lives. Not just the ones wealthy people are part of, or whose buildings sit on top of an oilfield or a goldmine.

God's children are heirs to things so precious that no amount of money can buy them. All they need is a tutor who sees their potential. That's *you* as a leader in the church. Your job is to *develop a culture* in which these young emerging leaders can mature to the point where they can steward the inheritance of Christ. Your church can have the best programs in the world, but deep-rooted change won't happen without the right culture shift.

> Your church can have the best programs in the world, but deep-rooted change won't happen without the right culture shift.

"But we don't have all the right resources," you say.

"But we don't have that kind of culture," you say.

"But you don't know our church and the leadership group we inherited," you say.

Ephesians 4:11 says the purpose of a leader is "for the equipping of the saints" (NASB), or "for building up the body of Christ" (NRSV). If you have people with Christ living inside, then you've got all you need. The right culture *can* be built by starting with what you already have.

David faced a similar situation. He certainly didn't start with a dream team: "Everyone who was in distress, and everyone who was in debt, and everyone who was discontented gathered to him; and he became captain over them" (1 Samuel 22:2).

> The right culture *can* be built by starting with what you already have.

From the roster of people who would never qualify as first-round draft choices, David built one of the best teams Israel ever knew. It seemed as though David's group should be called "the Losers," but by *changing their culture* David led them to become a championship team of guerilla warriors.

Suppose you're starting off as David did. Suppose you feel your best team is full of distressed and discontented people. How can you learn to steward the inheritance of your church? Let us show you, through what God has done in our churches.

WE STARTED THERE TOO: NEW HOPE'S MUSICIANS

At New Hope Christian Fellowship O'ahu in Hawaii, we're continually asked, "Where'd you get such great musicians? Did they migrate from other churches? How do you recruit such talented people?" It's understandable that they ask because our musicians are incredibly, amazingly good.

The answer is that they didn't come to New Hope fully assembled and ready to play. As a pioneer church, we knew we needed to build a culture where aspiring musicians would find an environment conducive to growth. So we built a culture that values musicians who are still in the early stages. Our keyboardist, Charlie, is twenty-one years old, but we believed in him when he was fourteen. Likewise, we believed in Teresa when she was sixteen. We believed in Errol when his family was falling apart, and we believed in Maria when she was not yet a Christian. (True situations, but the names have been changed.) Today, years later, look at all of them!

Heathcliff was a guitarist who had a dream of playing with one of New Hope's weekend worship teams, but he was afraid of making mistakes. Fear threw him off his confidence and distracted his motives. I sensed his desire to use his gifts for the Lord even though he was constantly being dissuaded by his fear, so I encouraged him to play anyway. "No way!" he replied. "I'd die! I just can't."

I pushed back on him. "Heathcliff, I want you to play with one stipulation: that you won't plug your guitar in."

His first response was, "That would be weird. No one will hear me!"

I replied, "One person will hear you—Jesus. When you are comfortable playing for an audience of One, then you'll be ready to play for an audience of many."

So he played without amplification, for six months. During that time he learned to play with excellence and without being intimidated. Today he is one of our stars.

We Started There Too: Fellowship Bible Fills Dreams, Not Slots

Fellowship Bible Church in Little Rock, Arkansas, has built a culture that invites people to use their gifts and allows them to step into new roles, knowing that we stand behind them. Our goal is to fill dreams, not slots.

Our goal is to fill dreams, not slots.

A great illustration at Fellowship is Jim Phillips, an accountant, and his wife, Connie. They came to me several years ago, expressing a desire to provide mentors and education that would counter the rampant sexual promiscuity sweeping through the junior high public schools. "I have this dream," Jim said, "but I don't know how."

With others they started an abstinence-based mentoring program called Excel. The church helped through encouragement, publicity, and small-group support. Now they're in every public school in central Arkansas. Some one thousand volunteers from 125 churches are mentoring ten thousand students in thirty-one public schools. They do all this with the support of a half-million-dollar budget and seven full-time staff. In an equipping culture that believes each person has gifts to be expressed, Jim and Connie have gone from taking a baby step to really making a difference in our community.

Nancy Carter became part of Fellowship years ago. Not long after, she sought help for her crumbling marriage; she found love and support from our people and staff. It became clear to Nancy that she would need to provide financially for her children, and when the staff receptionist position at our church came open we offered it to her and she accepted.

One day, when things were slow, one of the staff asked her to help create some posters for a church activity. Nancy's designs were so good that word got around about her artistic abilities. Soon she was being asked to do all kinds of artwork. We encouraged her to further the development of her abilities through computer training and other help. In time, we hired her to do media work for us. As our church grew, her media office became a department, which Nancy now leads. All this is because the culture of our church is to help people be the best they can be for the kingdom of God.

Tim Holder is another example. He came to Fellowship struggling with his sexual orientation. He was scared to death. But he found people who reached out to him. They gave him hope and courage. He opened up and shared his struggle, and people loved him even more. This love helped Tim take charge of his life, grow strong, and determine, regardless of his struggles, to be pure. Today, he is on our worship staff and engaged in leading our Recovery Ministry as a proven example of God's amazing grace.

No one plans transformations like this. The cultural soil at our churches makes it happen from the ground up. It grows people's lives from the inside out.

WHAT IS CULTURE?

Your culture is the lens through which you view your life. If you change the lens, you change your outlook. Change the culture, and everything else changes, including the future.

> Change the culture, and everything else changes, including the future.

A dictionary would define *culture* as the sum of attitudes, customs, and beliefs that distinguish one group of people from another. Its root meaning is shared with the word *agriculture,* referring to soil that has been tilled, and by extension a set of traits that have been plowed into a group's way of life. Culture is transmitted from one generation to the next through language, material objects, ritual, institutions, and art.

On most computers, everything that happens is filtered through Microsoft Windows. Those "windows" are the lens through which everything on your computer is translated. Likewise, one social scientist says culture is the shared software of our minds.[1]

QUICK FIXERS VS. CULTURE GROWERS

A young woman at New Hope O'ahu became ill. As many of us would do, she visited a doctor, got diagnosed, went to a pharmacy, and began taking the prescribed antibiotic. She felt better for several days but then became worse. She went back to the doctor, who made another diagnosis and sent her home with another prescription. Again she had symptoms of health for a few days but then became ill.

> Culture is the shared software of our minds.
> (Geert Hofstede)

The cycle continued until finally her doctors discovered they were treating her for the wrong thing. She had an abscessed cyst in her fallopian tube. The doctors had every good and noble intention, but until they dealt with the real problem she was actually becoming worse, even though each shot of antibiotics gave a short-term appearance of health. It was like hoping to lose weight by sometimes eating less of the wrong things.

Too many churches operate the same way. When something is wrong, we try to get it fixed, but like Travis in the opening story the real problem remains unchanged.

Want to change the future of your church for the better? Begin by acknowledging that even though you've been working hard in your church, you're treating symptoms with the wrong prescriptions. It starts with acknowledging that regardless of how your church looks now, it has billion-dollar potential. The potential is found in your culture—the *real and true* culture of your church, not the quick-fix culture you may so often be tempted to try. It all starts when you, along with other church leaders, accept that your key role is to be the tutor who stewards a culture that releases this deep spiritual potential into the lives of your people.

Culture Shift asks you to ignore the quick-fix programs that are all around you and, working from the inside out, grow your culture into the rich inheritance God wants to provide. If you're ready for that, let's move on.

· · · · ·

Each chapter of *Culture Shift* readily lends itself to discussion and application, and you are invited to create follow-up exercises from each chapter. The main sections that invite active participation, however, are in Chapters Four, Five, and Six, where you are guided in identifying the culture of your church and then exploring the next specific transition steps that are needed.

Your Destiny in Seed Form

E ARLY IN MY MINISTRY, YEARS BEFORE I CAME TO New Hope Christian Fellowship O'ahu in Hawaii, I traveled to many churches on behalf of Youth for Christ. We had our first child at the time, and my wife, Anna, would take precious little Amy to the church nursery. She discreetly tried to discern if they possessed the two basic prerequisites that she as a mother required to give her the confidence and security to leave our newborn: Was the place clean? More important, did the attendants really love kids?

Anna observed some terrible environments: "Child number four, sit down! Child number three, are you wet again? Seven, seven, don't bite number twelve!" Whenever she found herself in a nursery of that sort, where they treated children like numbers instead of people, she'd bring Amy with her into the sanctuary and care for our child herself. As a good parent who loves children, Anna had no desire to entrust Amy to a nursery that could not provide adequate nurturing and care.

This observation taught me something: a church is like a nursery for the spiritual babies God the Father is drawing. He is constantly calling people into the nursery. The Bible's message is clear: "No one can come to Me unless the Father who sent Me draws him" (John 6:44). And the Father is not done yet!

God began filling nurseries on the very first day of the New Testament church: "And the Lord was adding to their number day by day those who were being saved" (Acts 2:47). His desire is that his church, like a great banquet hall, "may be full" (Luke 14:23). Indeed, heaven will be populated "from every tribe and tongue and people and nation" (Revelation 5:9).

God is a good parent who loves his children, and he doesn't want to send his newborns just anywhere. It pains him for them to be in a neglected environment, or one that has posted the equivalent of a No Vacancy sign. Why send people with great potential into a culture where they cannot grow and become fruitful? However, if a church offers a rich, healthy, inspiring culture that gladly accepts those whom God is drawing, then he has armloads of young, yet-to-be-developed D. L. Moodys, Mother Teresas, and others to bring. But they're all in seed form as babies.

> When a church offers a culture that gladly accepts those whom God is drawing, then he has armloads of future leaders to bring.

We've got to do the long-term work of building a nursery—that is, a culture—in which these future leaders can thrive. We've got to commit ourselves to a long-term organic approach of life-on-life ministry that unleashes authentic kingdom values into people's lives.

In the late 1960s and early 1970s, Little Rock, Arkansas, was mired in what could be called "cultural Christianity." As part of America's Southern Bible belt, the city boasted churches all over the place. But for many, Christianity was measured more by church attendance than by any life-altering pursuit of Jesus. Instead, our city, scarred by racial hurt and deeply divided by prejudice and politics, was marked by a formal religion practiced mostly on Sunday mornings. The impact of the gospel rarely seemed to spill over into the daily life of our community.

During this same time, a group of students at the University of Arkansas, none of whom had given much thought to God or his plan in their lives, came to a vital faith through the ministry of Campus Crusade for Christ. Their fellowship was deep and passionate. After college, many of these babes in Christ came to Little Rock but struggled to find a church home that encouraged the same level of spiritual fervor and excitement they had experienced in college. Where was a spiritual nursery that God could send them to?

They talked with one another and began to search God's word for direction. They reflected on the "different vision" God had given them for a church and what a real Christian community could be about. Through faith they saw and tasted the future, even though it wasn't there.

In 1977, about twenty individuals began meeting in each other's homes to further develop the sense of Christian community that God had used to transform so many of them. That fall they became a new church, meeting in a small elementary school. It was a setting that appropriately matched this small, now elementary-aged group of believers. Eventually they became Fellowship Bible Church. When they decided to bring in additional leadership to help them further develop their ideals, I was one of those they called to lead this young church.

> Through faith they saw and tasted the future, even though it wasn't there.

From our experience together and vision of what could be, we slowly cultivated a culture where people lived out their faith, cared for one another and for the poor and needy, shared their faith with others, and built spiritual bridges into the community. Through the resultant growth, we came to realize that what Jesus said was true: a healthy church culture is almost irresistible (Matthew 5:16).

As God's purposes became flesh in the lives of the people in our congregation, with all its imperfections, we saw something we had difficulty understanding. It seemed incredibly simple: as newcomers put their seed in our soil, they grew. Roy Rainey, an older gentleman who recently joined Fellowship, put it this way: "You can't help but catch the spirit of this church!"

As You Awaken *to* Culture, Remember *to* Focus *on* Kingdom Values

Our starting point at Fellowship Bible (the same is true for New Hope) was not a statement that we want to create a new culture. Instead, it was simply a desire to move more toward a focus on kingdom values. It was a matter of getting in touch with what God wanted us to be, in attitude as well as behavior, seeing it with the eyes of faith— what it might look like in a particular locality—working hard to embody those values as best we could, and then beginning to let those values, through us, change our locality.

Without a biblical basis anchoring it to kingdom values, any church is likely to hit trouble. It's so easy to drift (Hebrews 2:1) or delude ourselves (2 Corinthians 11:3) as church leaders, and even with the best of intentions we might move toward darkness rather than light. Once you lose your biblical bearings, you have no idea who you really are. As Paul warns, "Don't let the world around you squeeze you into its mold, but let God remold your minds from within . . ." (Romans 12:2, Phillips).

In Greek mythology, the god Prometheus was a troublemaker. He could change his identity into a tree, a horse, or anything else in order to trick his friends. He turned into so many shapes that one day he couldn't find his way back to who he was. He had forgotten.

Some churches are like that. Having chased so many dreams of others, they lose their true sense of self. We want to make sure we're not Promethean ministries who change, change, and change until we don't remember what our defining purpose is.

When asked what's distinctive about their culture, people in too many churches admit, "I don't know." Or worse, they define their church's identity by cloning the latest program that's hot on the direct-mail or conference circuit.

It's easier to duplicate than to incarnate.

If we follow the pack, we often bypass the incarnational power the Lord can provide. If we're not careful and continue to clone ourselves with a string of programs from other churches, we may forget who we are and lose our identity. We become only a shell without true spiritual substance.

Instead, we want to help you create a culture that is distinctly and unmistakably your own. Then, if you drift (and you will, as both of us have from time to time) your church's own, strong cultural anchor will pull you safely back.

VALUE-DRIVEN VS. PROGRAM-DRIVEN

During my years at Fellowship Bible Church in Little Rock, I've learned a painful lesson: ultimately our church culture resides not in buildings, programs, or printed proclamations but in people who say, "This is what God wants us to become." The personal pain in this lesson is that I can't merely talk about an idea. I must embody it. I have to communicate it through relationships and specific examples. Otherwise no one truly gets it.

This insight came together for me in regard to something quite simple. I was reflecting on the first impression guests receive when they first arrive on our campus for worship. I was concerned about how unkempt our grounds looked. "That's just not us," I thought. "It doesn't reflect our values or the way we do ministry here." I decided to mention the matter to a team at the church. "We need to keep our property looking sharp so that when someone comes here their first reaction will be positive and expectant," I said.

But nobody got it. At least not the way I was envisioning.

Then I took a walk with Ann Blair, who was serving at the time as our facilities team leader. I pointed out my concerns to her as we looked at a specific area of our property together. "This is what we could do here," I said, highlighting a few ideas where we could make major improvements.

"Why do that?" she asked.

So I explained. I linked my comments to our vision and values as a church. Then we walked to another area and had a similar exchange.

Over the course of several conversations, Ann came to understand and appreciate the environment I was trying to communicate.

I had certain ideals in mind, such as excellence and quality. She is an intelligent person and speaks the same Southern dialect of English that I do, but we didn't connect, until I gave her specific examples—models—of what my ideals might look like in our context and why.

Ann was soon off and running, able to make independent "that is us" or "that is *not* us" decisions, and even to convey our culture on her own to others.

> The cultural epicenter of a church is a person or team you trust to apply biblical principles to your specific context.

The "a-ha!" for me was the realization that the cultural epicenter of a church is not a static code or rules, but life-on-life equipping that ultimately allows a person or team you trust to apply biblical principles to your specific context. There are few experiences I love better than observing a team meeting where leaders whom I have mentored take principles I've taught them from the Bible and apply them to their ministry, using their unique spiritual gifts in the process.

This is how a church culture is unleashed! Kingdom values plus today's world plus human personality. It's a linkage that allows a church to be value-driven rather than program-driven.

Change *the* Culture *to* Release Your Future

By addressing the importance of culture first, you are releasing your church's future. Just as a small mustard seed thrown into good soil becomes the largest shrub around, on inhospitable ground it is choked to death before things can even get started (Matthew 13:6, 22, 31–32).

A church's culture represents the intersection of three values you're to steward: God's kingdom agenda, who you are, and your unique setting. These are the foundational elements of a church's culture. When church leaders get in touch with God's kingdom culture, begin to live it, and figure out how it can be expressed in their locality, then a new, rich culture inevitably emerges.

God's Kingdom Agenda

To enter God's kingdom is to come under the redemptive rule and reign of God. To be a part of God's kingdom—God's royal rule, which includes eternal life—means we are being called to constant life change.

God's kingdom is so valuable and such a priority that we pursue it as we would a costly pearl or hidden treasure (Matthew 13:44–45). According to Jesus, the kingdom's first demand is that we "repent and believe the gospel" (Matthew 4:17; Mark 1:15). After we "enter into the kingdom of God" (John 3:5), our relationship with God changes, as do the noticeable ways we treat others; the Sermon on the Mount illustrates this well (Matthew 5:1–7:29).

Culture represents the intersection of three values you're to steward: God's kingdom agenda, who you are, and your unique setting.

In fact, kingdom living affects our attitude toward all of life; for example, we become characterized by trust rather than fear (Luke 13:18–20), a spirit of forgiveness toward others (Matthew 18:23), and a uniqueness that makes us distinct as representatives of Jesus, the "light of the world" (John 8:12; Matthew 5:14). Life in the kingdom is one of "righteousness and peace and joy in the Holy Spirit" (Roman 14:17). Only in God's kingdom do humans find fulfillment of their desire for righteousness, justice, peace, joy, freedom from sin and guilt, and a restored relationship to God.

God's kingdom sets the agenda for the church; in light of God's kingdom agenda, everything we do at church—including what we think and who we are—is kingdom culture building. It's preparing the tarmac and lighting pattern at an airport, like wilderness missionaries cutting back overgrowth and

God's kingdom sets the agenda for the church; everything we do at church is kingdom culture building.

making a landing strip open and available. If we can do that for our churches, hundreds of people will come and land.

Too often, however, a church misses the mark by following a misguided agenda. Sometimes we're more interested in marketing than in modeling kingdom values. Sometimes as leaders our need for the spotlight overrides what's best for our people. We can begin unknowingly to build a culture erected around us. A little success can quickly seduce us into feeling it's all about "me." In contrast, Rick Warren begins *The Purpose-Driven Life* with these wise words: "It's not about you. The purpose of your life is far greater than your own personal fulfillment, your peace of mind, or even your happiness. It's far greater than your family, your career, or even your wildest dreams and ambitions. If you want to know why you were placed on this planet, you must begin with God. You were born *by* his purpose and *for* his purpose."[1]

In this world, by contrast, we like to take credit by saying, "Notice me" or "I did that." Our mentality is to look for our fifteen minutes of fame. One danger of being absorbed by the world is that we take on its thinking process. When we do, the things of God don't make sense because we have a different sense of payback. The challenge of kingdom leadership is to learn how to live humbly in the world, discerning what is consistent with God's kingdom, as if to "extract the precious from the worthless" (Jeremiah 15:19) and then courageously, for the glory of God, going there.

WHO WE ARE

As the Holy Spirit mentors us in how to change the culture of our churches, all of our insight on our destiny starts with our relationship with God and God's Word, the Holy Scriptures. Thus it's vitally important for church leaders to stay in the Word of God, as is emphasized in Acts 6:2 and elsewhere.

Time listening to God and in Scripture repatterns how we feel and think about others. It transforms and renews our own mind, and we receive the very mind of Christ. We begin to respond as Jesus would, just as Scripture calls for: "Have this attitude in yourselves which was also in Christ Jesus" (Philippians 2:5). People say, "You've been hanging around with Jesus."

Suppose you want to learn how to play blues on the guitar. You sign up for once-a-week lessons at your nearby community college. You sit with a class of a hundred other students, learning at the speed of the slowest student. The instructor, though entirely capable, moves the class forward to the next principle or skill only after everyone has caught on to the previous one.

Unknown to you, B. B. King, the world-famous blues guitarist, happens to live in your town. He walks by the classroom, watches for a while, and decides that you have great potential. So after class he makes you an incredible offer: Would you like a daily lesson from him, free of charge? The choice is a no-brainer, between a weekly slow-paced community college lesson and personalized daily tutoring from a master musician.

After two years of daily mentoring from King, you are not only playing well but are also informally teaching a group of others what you've learned about playing guitar. Your old community college teacher observes you and says, "You didn't learn this from me. You've been hanging around a master."

Authentic, spiritual leaders, trained and equipped by the Master of the universe, not only live well; they make it their priority to serve others so as to help them discover the same thing. They have grasped the idea of other people's potential in seed form. These leaders know how to start with seeds. They understand there is no substitute for personal life-on-life ministry. They are able to cultivate a culture that nourishes those believers to grow up and blossom with all the beauty and fruitfulness that God intends.

OUR UNIQUE SETTING

Your church's context is one of a kind. The language needed to verbalize and live out the gospel has certain nuances particular to your church alone. The appeal of the mass-produced church is over, if it ever existed. One of your greatest challenges as a leader is to unlearn any inappropriate preconceptions and develop a culture that best models the maturity of what it means to be in Christ (see Ephesians 4:12–16).

In *UnLearning Church,* Michael Slaughter speaks of the kind of leaders needed for tomorrow's church: "Their commonality is that they excel in local implementation. They connect people in their community or culture to an experience of God, to authentic community, and to life purpose. They're radically local within the same city, but reaching distinctly different people groups. If the emerging church is recognized and valued for anything, it's for a highly effective, indigenous carrying out of the mission of Jesus Christ."[2]

Every church requires a certain unique culture. God knows that. He has called specific people together in specific churches for specific reasons. He doesn't just throw us together in a church at random. All of us are like pieces of a giant jigsaw puzzle that only he fully understands. Nevertheless, if church leadership listens to God's Word, serves God's people, and is sensitive to the community it resides in, then a clear picture of who Jesus is for that local setting is powerfully revealed.

> God has called specific people together in specific churches for specific reasons.

If you determine for your church that this future is what you believe God wants for you tomorrow, then you can know how to start sowing today. Remember the mustard seed? Your responsibility as steward is to ensure that you sow the seed in the richest, best-tilled soil you can so it has everything it needs to grow to the fullest potential.

What You Think
Is What You See

YOU'VE PROBABLY HEARD THE SAYING, "SOW A THOUGHT, you'll reap a desire. Sow that desire enough, you'll reap an action. Sow that action enough, you'll reap a habit. Sow a habit, you'll reap your destiny." It all begins with a thought: how you think about your church determines what you see and the culture you create.

> How you think about your church determines what you see and the culture you create.

Years ago, I pastored a church in Hilo, the easternmost city on the island of Hawaii. Six months into the ministry, we held a churchwide picnic. I was having a great time until a man with a condescending tone struck up a conversation. "Do you know what kind of people you have in this church?" he said.

"Nice ones?" I replied with a smile.

He didn't laugh. In fact, he grimaced. Then he growled, "They're sick," he said. "I've been here a long time and I know them."

He began to give me a verbal tour through the congregation. He first pointed to a teenager. "That girl was raised by a mentally retarded grandmother because her own mother abandoned her," he said. "She does strange things."

Then he pointed out a young man. "That guy is on crack," he said, "and that one is on probation. He has to go back to jail each weekend. Better watch him."

Pointing to another cluster of people, he said, "That couple is living together, and that guy has a bad swindling problem. He can tap the church coffers, and you'll never know it."

After offering a similar commentary on other members, he looked at me and sighed. "They're sick here! Your church is full of sickies!" he said. Then he walked off.

I was speechless. I had thought they were wonderful people! But after his eye-opening narration, I started looking at them through other eyes. "That girl *does* act a bit strange at times," I observed. I also began to wonder about the guy standing near her, the one on probation. "His eyes *are* shifty," I thought. Frustrated with my new findings, I argued with God. "You gave me a bunch of sickies!" I protested. "They're *all* sick!"

When I finally stopped whining and started listening, God corrected me. It was as if he said to my heart, "I didn't come for well people, but for those who are ailing." I remembered what Jesus said: "It is not those who are healthy who need a physician, but those who are sick; I did not come to call the righteous, but sinners" (Mark 2:17).

The Lord seemed to quietly continue: "So don't you be ashamed of them! I need them to be restored, and if you can't restore them in a congregation called New Hope Christian Fellowship, I need to find another nursery. I'm calling you to love them because I love them."

God seemed to have more to say. "And I'm not ashamed of you, Wayne Cordeiro—and you're a sickie too!"

God nailed me. I realized that we're all wounded. I have two choices. I can view these people as a bunch of losers, destined always to remain that way. Or I can bring them into God's embrace and they'll be healed, allowing God's power to be "perfected in weakness" (2 Corinthians 12:9).

What I think about my church determines what I see. It determines the kind of culture we foster. My choice is to view the church as a hospital where needy people (that's all of us!) are getting well.

How can you and the leaders of your church make your own what-kind-of-culture-will-we-have decision? It may seem obvious at first, but as you dig deeper you'll find it's not that easy.

Most of us would prefer to start working with ready-made, mature, veteran Christians—the kind who have a wonderful attitude, are genuinely helpful, and are already capable of reproducing themselves. Who would turn down a crop of Spirit-empowered leaders like that? As Carl George points out, the need for leaders of this caliber is the biggest ministry cap in most churches: "The creation of pastoral, ministry-capable leadership must become the core value of the church of the future, second only to listening to God."[1]

The next part of the decision is harder. What if God wants to send you other types of people as well? "What am I going to do with everyone else?" God may ask.

Maybe you're willing to extend a bit. "OK, we'll take some new Christians," you offer to God. "Hopefully they won't take too much maintenance."

But God still isn't done. "What am I going to do with everyone else?" he asks again.

Hmmm. "Like who?"

"How open are you to non-Christian seekers? Will you accept those who say, 'I don't know the Lord, but I need help'?"

"Sure," you agree.

Then God declares: "Good, you got the nice ones. Now, how about wounded people who have lost their way home? What about people who need to be restored and healed? How about closed-minded non-Christians who say, 'I don't like church'?"

The list could go on and on.

Our point is this: the church is a place for people to be restored into God's image (Colossians 3:10). Therefore the church is not to be a come-to-hide community, but a come-to-be-restored environment.

We embrace people with all their warts and foibles. We don't say "Get your life together first and then come to church" but rather "Come and belong, and get your lives together inside God's embrace."

A lot of people out there need help on their journey. Some are open but are waiting to be convinced before they'll be willing to find their way back to God. Some are broken and need to experience Christ's patience and care through us.

How do *you* look at things? If you look through the lens of a pessimist, you won't see much hope. If you're insecure, you will not see many options for empowerment. If you're embarrassed by your congregation, you won't know how to help them. The culture you create is largely a product of how you see those whom God has placed you with.

Culture shapes the church, and leaders make the culture.

You have to think rightly in order to lead well. What your mind dwells upon determines your vantage point, and your vantage point as a leader affects the culture you shape. Culture shapes the church, and leaders make the culture.

You Might Need *to* Repent

During a difficult time at that same church in Hilo, "Billy" talked to me incessantly about his kid, his dog, and just about everything else. He never seemed to stop.

I grew tired of his ramblings, and finally I ran out of patience. Whenever I saw him coming, I'd duck into the bathroom and wait until he went away.

One night he called me and blathered for almost an hour. I even set the phone down momentarily to answer the door, and he never knew it. Once in a while I'd interject "Hallelujah!" or "Yes, God is good"—primarily to make him think I was interested. In reality, I was only tolerating his love of hearing his own voice.

After I hung up the phone, I said out loud, "What a bonehead!"

Then I heard from the Lord.

The Lord convicted me down to my socks. It felt as if God said, "Wayne, do you know the reason I'm not blessing the church? It's because you think its people are boneheads."

Uh-oh.

The Lord continued, "Your response shows what you really think. You're trying to live up to an image of a tolerant pastor, but in your heart you think people are boneheads. Because of that, I can't bless your work among them."

I dropped to my knees and repented. "O God, please forgive me."

I began to pray words that I still pray regularly to this day, adapted from David: "Let the words of my mouth and the meditation of my heart be acceptable in Your sight, O Lord, my rock and my Redeemer" (Psalm 19:14).

In my daily prayers I say, "Father, may my thoughts please you today. Use my thoughts only for your purposes, and let them be dedicated to You and You alone." I then begin to work on my thoughts so that at the end of the day, my thoughts will have pleased the Lord. As my thoughts become the mind of Christ, my actions please God as well. My ideal is to model David, who God described as "a man whose heart beats to my heart, a man who will do what I tell him" (Acts 13:22, The Message).

CHANGE YOUR THINKING *to* CHANGE YOUR VISION

Do you know that we actually see with our brain, not with our eyes? The eye is simply a lens that captures an image that our brain defines. It adds history and associations, all of which are seasoning that can be shaped by the Word of God. So let your brain soak up the Word of God; it will strongly color what you see.

Jesus reminds us that "The eye is the lamp of the body; so then if your eye is clear, your whole body will be full of light. But if your eye is bad, your whole body will be full of darkness. If then the light that is in you is darkness, how great is the darkness!" (Matthew 6:22–23). Changing our mind determines how we see.

What you look at, what you think about, and what you mull over color your life and paint your perspective. This is why the Scripture says: "We fix our eyes on not what is seen, but on what is unseen. For what is seen is temporary, but what is unseen is eternal" (2 Corinthians 4:18).

The Word of God wants to teach us how to see, according to the Apostle Paul: "I pray that the eyes of your heart may be enlightened, so that you will know what is the hope of His calling, what are the riches of the glory of His inheritance in the saints, and what is the surpassing greatness of His power toward us who believe" (Ephesians 1:18–19).

We must soak up the right things in order to perceive correctly: "Whatever is true, whatever is honorable, whatever is right, whatever is pure, whatever is lovely, whatever is of good repute, if there is any excellence and if anything worthy of praise, dwell on these things. The things you have learned and received and heard and seen in me, practice these things, and the God of peace will be with you" (Philippians 4:8–9).

Repeat this thought process, whether with good thoughts or bad, and you develop a template. The template then develops attitude, which develops your disposition, which determines your character . . . which determines your future. The book *Attitudes That Attract Success*[2] by Wayne Cordeiro says that your attitude is your second most important decision in life; it's second only to your decision on whether to become a follower of Jesus Christ. Second is the attitude with which you follow him.

FREEDOM *to* INNOVATE

As you begin to awaken to the possibilities of your own culture, you notice a wonderful freedom to innovate. Innovation that looks for ways to make the soil richer is very important. When a church has a rich culture, it's usually being produced by people who have been thinking about how to make the existing soil better.

Ask questions that go to the heart of the issue: What are our true needs in this church? How can we *best* meet those needs? How can we truly serve people? What can we do to bring out the best in our people? Simply thinking seriously about these questions creates space for people to grow.

> When a church has a rich culture, it's usually being produced by people who have been thinking about how to make the existing soil better.

It's important to allow yourself *not* to have all the answers at first. Why? Because the answer varies from setting to setting, and from one season to another. Be innovative! What works in a season of drought doesn't necessarily work when you have too much rain. What works in spring doesn't necessarily work in winter. What allowed people to flourish in the Spirit ten years ago might be spiritually strangulating today. Always be on the lookout for how you can customize your programs to keep people growing.

What worked at your last church may not work at your present church. At Fellowship Bible Church, for example, my thinking is entirely different from how I thought at the first church I served. Long ago, my question was, "How do we build a big church?" Back then, I didn't understand the releasing power of culture.

Today, I'm looking for how to unleash people. In fact, this value is a strong part of our culture at Fellowship. Fellowship displays a sense of unity and harmony I couldn't imagine in my previous church; the ripple effect of our unleashing culture has extended our church's touch to areas where my lack of personal relationships means I'll never be able to reach: to poor kids downtown, faculty

> Leaders who think seriously about what brings out the best in people create space for people to grow.

members of the medical school here in town, business leaders, and more.

Here's how it happens. Because our people are thinking of how they can be unleashed for the kingdom, *they* become creative. It's not just me doing all the work. Each and every member is turning over the soil, making it more fertile. They are creating good soil, and more and more seeds are sprouting in places I would never have imagined.

These metrics of kingdom growth are solidly biblical, and freeing to me personally. Great churches grow by thinking prayerfully and organically. When people care about people, everyone does his or her best to unleash others. The more the church's leadership fosters an environment of rich textures like this, the easier it is for others to become creative as well. Certainly you need somewhere to meet as a church and some degree of organization, but without the freedom to innovate your church will always end up short.

Like improvisation in a jazz ensemble, "the next five measures are yours" is a wonderfully liberating way to do church.

In short, innovation creates space to make the play. It gives room for purposeful creative strategies to emerge. It's like improvisation in a jazz ensemble: the soloist needs to stay consistent with the rhythm and true to the melody in some way, but for five measures the musician is free to play notes that come straight from the heart. "The next five measures are yours" is a wonderfully liberating way to do church.

GOOD THINKING LEADS *to* MOMENTUM

Jim Collins, a former professor at Stanford Business School and the best-selling author of several business books, notably *Good to Great,*[3] has discovered that most great businesses are piloted not by charismatic celebrity leaders but by leaders who figure out the right thing to do. According to Collins and his research team, leaders who take their companies from good to great possess a unique blend of humility and resolve. This kind of leader focuses on what needs to be done, gets behind it, and enlists the whole organization to help push it, until it finally makes one "rotation." As Collins phrases it, "Picture a . . . massive metal disk mounted horizontally on an axle, about 30 feet in diameter, 2 feet thick, and weighing about 5,000 pounds. Now imagine that your task is to get that flywheel rotating on the axle as fast and long as possible."[4] With some initial momentum, the next rotation comes a little easier. It's the same with the rotation after that, "turn upon turn, building momentum until a point of breakthrough, and beyond."[5] Before long, repeated rotations are producing an incredible success. But the movement started with sheer commitment to the right value.

Church culture is like that. Wise thinking leads to doing the right spiritual things, while resolute determination leads to staying behind those things until the effort finally births a new culture. The new culture then begins to give life to everything it touches.

Christian shepherds with leadership gifts should be called upon to identify the primary flywheels of their church's culture. These main gears are the ones that trigger other gears. Whatever the configuration of the secondary gears, if the main gear stops hundreds of other gears stop. If the main gear cranks, the machine keeps moving.

> The new culture begins to give life to everything it touches.

On the other hand, a small gear can stop or break and the others will keep cranking. Many times pastors and other church leaders put time, energy, and finances into the wrong gears—our pet ones—and we miss what the main gears are.

Certainly a church is a Spirit-empowered organism and not a lifeless machine, but it's essential for leaders to find the right wheels to turn. They do so by identifying the main gears of greatest spiritual value and strategic influence (worship services, discipleship, leadership development ministries, and so on) and then giving their time and energy to bless, affirm, and deepen these areas.

FREEDOM *to* TAKE RISKS *of* FAITH

We must always include faith in transforming our thinking. The Bible's constant message is, "As is your faith . . ." We don't want to limit God. We are often the determiner of how much God can do through our life and church. Whatever God wants our church to be, we can be and do.

Moses was walking along in the desert when he saw a burning bush. He noticed that "the bush was burning with fire, yet the bush was not consumed" (Exodus 3:2). The Lord, not the bush, was providing the flame. God was providing its power.

Was there anything special about that one bush? Could God have used any bush? Absolutely; any bush will do when God is providing the firepower.

We're all like bushes. God can use us, because the burning impulse comes from him, not us. Any bush will do if God adds the light.

NOW, FOLLOW YOUR THINKING

Whatever God is giving you as your dream, tell yourself that you can do it. As Paul affirmed, "I can do all things through Him who strengthens me" (Philippians 4:13).

Passages such as Matthew 9:29 remind us that "it shall be done to you according to your faith." If you're waiting for more faith, start with what you have—but don't limit God. God isn't looking for talented people so much as for available people.

The Apostle Peter had to learn this lesson as he built a culture in which his fellow Jews would become followers of Jesus. God had assigned Peter with a responsibility to preach the gospel to the Jews. That dream was shattered when he was arrested, put into prison, bound with chains, and assigned to a squad of soldiers who guarded him (Acts 12:5 ff.). He must have thought he was at a dead end.

Then, when God's intervention came, Peter did not know that a miracle was happening. Fortunately, when the angel showed up, Peter didn't say, "Hey, that bright light really bothers my eyes. I'm really tired tonight and I don't know who you are, but if this is a God thing, *you* do it. I'm going back to sleep." Instead, he cooperated.

A protracted miracle often requires your cooperation at every point. The Lord's reason for showing you a dream isn't necessarily so that you will initiate it. Maybe he's merely informing you and wants someone else to bring it to pass, as with David constructing a temple. Others, like Joseph, spoke too soon of the dream God had given him.

When adversity arises and it seems you've hit a wall, it doesn't mean the dream is over. Sometimes God has to wrest it out of our hands, and the only way he can do so is to shatter it like pottery. Our role is to stay faithful in adversity: "Put on your sandals," "Don't be afraid," "Follow me," "Walk past those terrifying guards," and "Go down the next streets on your own." When you are in the midst of a miracle, God's part is to bring it to pass. Our part is to follow.

> When you are in the midst of a miracle, God's part is to bring it to pass. Our part is to follow.

When God calls you to become a change agent, he often starts by changing how you think. He expects you to respond in obedience and faith. Those elements become part of the new culture that you create.

Birthing the Culture

THE TRIP FROM HAWAII TO A CERTAIN CITY
in China initially made me feel that our coun-
tries are close to each other. But through what happened next, I discovered that we are worlds apart.

They arrived at the nondescript apartment individually and in pairs, watching carefully to detect
any secret police who might be tailing them. Several
had scars on their hands or necks from being shack-
led and mistreated for their faith. Yet none seemed
to be fearful. Instead, a sense of peace, quiet joy, and
spiritual expectation filled the room as they entered.
Although I did not speak their language, their lives
clearly conveyed a powerful and inviting quality.

Soon all eighteen of them had arrived. Each is
an overseer in an underground house church movement, all from the same section of a country where
Christianity is illegal.

I asked our translator to find out how many
people they oversaw. After three or four minutes of

discussion they had an answer: about twenty-two million. My jaw visibly dropped in astonishment and admiration.

They immediately put me to work. They had me start teaching early each morning and continue, virtually nonstop, all day long in our hot, crowded room. They had traveled at least thirteen difficult hours by train and now sat all day long on hardwood floors.

When I asked that a Scripture passage be read from Bibles we had brought in their language, several quoted the verses from memory. I later learned that many had memorized entire books of the Bible while in prison, risking further abuse if they were caught. "They can confiscate pages of Bibles that we may smuggle into prison," one woman explained to me, "but they can't take away that which is hidden in my heart. So whenever someone slipped me a page from a Bible, I memorized it and then passed it on to someone else."

I learned that if any of these people were caught at our training event, the minimum penalty would be three years in prison. (My only penalty would be immediate deportation from their country.) I found out that fifteen of the eighteen had already been imprisoned for their faith, one for twelve years. Another of them, who publishes a Christian newspaper, which is illegal, mentioned that he could not go home after our meetings. "The secret police are watching my house, planning to catch and arrest me," he explained.

"Are you sure this risk is worth it to you?" I asked at one point. "The police could break in these doors right now."

"If you will teach us for our two remaining days," they replied immediately, "we will stay here and learn."

At the conclusion of our time together, I asked how I might pray for them.

"Pray that we will become like you in America," one of them said. "You have many Bibles, freedom to worship openly, and even air conditioning to keep you from being distracted."

"No," I replied, convinced that I should be sitting on the floor and that *they* should be teaching me. "Instead, I will pray that *we* become like *you*."

• • • • •

Their churches must be a delight to our heavenly Father, for they have learned to incarnate a compelling, irresistible church culture. I want those same qualities to be birthed in us as well.

Your church can develop kingdom values with a fervency that matches these leaders of an underground church. But it won't happen if you're content with the status quo, or if you don't know how to lead your church to embody kingdom values. This second part of *Culture Shift* walks you through the process: identifying your church's unique culture and "totems," shifting the culture, and partnering with the Holy Spirit each step of the way.

Totems

Identifying Your Church's Culture

EVEN IF *YOU* HAVE NOT YET IDENTIFIED YOUR church's culture, others have. Culture announces its identity through everything you do. The values of your culture—stated or unstated, thought out or unintentional—shape the feel, behavior, and attitude of a congregation more than anything else.

Even if you have not yet identified your church's culture, others have.

How well have you identified *your* church's culture? If you don't take the time to identify its dominant values, you won't be able to evaluate whether they're the values you really intend to express. Nor will you be able to check your alignment. For instance, how consistent are these values for yourself, for your congregation, and for all those with whom your church comes in contact?

TOTEMS SYMBOLIZE YOUR CORE VALUES

Symbolic representations are quite common for expressing the values of various cultures and religions across the world. When the ancient Israelites entered the Promised Land by miraculously crossing the river

Jordan, for example, they erected a pile of stones where they camped that night. The memorial was designed, as the Lord explained through Joshua, to be "a sign . . . when your children ask later, saying, 'What do these stones mean to you?'" (Joshua 4:6).

The *mezuzah,* a small cylinder affixed to a doorpost, is an ancient symbol that signifies a Jewish family lives or works within. Inside the cylinder is a small piece of rolled-up parchment containing Deuteronomy 6:4–9 and 11:13–21, verses instructing the Israelites to teach God's commands to their children with diligence, talking of them "when you sit in your house and when you walk by the way and when you lie down and when you rise up" (Deuteronomy 6:7)—even writing them "on the doorposts of your house" (Deuteronomy 6:9).

You may never have noticed these small symbols, but in Alaska the Native American totem poles—with their enormous and colorful carved heads of eagles and salmon and bears—are hard to ignore. Each animal carved on the high wooden pole is a "totem"—an animal that embodies skills and values the tribe needs if it is to overcome and thrive in this hostile and challenging environment: "We must be wise as an owl, cunning as a fox, strong as a bear, resourceful as a badger, and persevering as a salmon that swims up the river." The totem pole, planted prominently in the village, announces to residents and strangers alike, "This is our culture. This is who we are."

> The totem pole announces to residents and strangers alike, "This is our culture. This is who we are."

The underlying message of any such symbol—be it a mezuzah, a totem animal, or a crucifix—is profound: "Don't forget who you are." It also serves specifically as a foundational ideal for the generations to come.

In this book we are using the term *totem* to help you identify your values and make them seen and heard. Silent but powerful, these values remind people in the most positive way of who they are and who they can be.

We, as leaders, can put them to good use. In a native Alaskan community, for example, a teenage boy might announce, "I'm leaving. Life is too hard here. I can't handle all the pressures of becoming an adult in this community."

An elder will take him to the center of the village. "See the salmon on that totem pole? That's us. The salmon doesn't give up; he swims upstream, even though it's difficult, until he reaches his goal. The salmon teaches us who we are: people who persevere and grow stronger through our struggle, and keep the generations going."

Likewise, we suggest that churches too can use a metaphorical totem to picture their core spiritual values and practices, signifying their culture and the atmosphere they want to build. These totems are the guiding values that birth the unique culture of a church.

Your particular church may differ from ours, just as Robert's and Wayne's differ from one another. New Hope's totems, for example, are heart for the lost, commitment to doing church as a team, a priority of developing and deploying emerging leaders, graciousness in all our dealings, uncompromising devotion to God's Word, and the discipline of living heart-first. The primary totems at Fellowship Bible are living winsome lives, equipping everyone to serve, modeling team ministry, really doing evangelism, building relevance and excellence into everything, connecting with the community, and multiplying through church planting. (We'll look at these in detail in Parts Three and Four.)

> Totems are the guiding spiritual values that birth the unique culture of a church.

Remembering Who You Are

The leaders of a community establish the culture that people grow up in. Israelites did it, the native Alaskans did it, and we in the church must do so as well. Whenever we cease to live the values we say we believe in, we destroy that culture and create one that's less inspiring, less transformational, and less authentic.

In Deuteronomy, chapters six and eight, God reminds his people, "When you get into the Promised Land, don't forget who you are." In

New Testament times, Paul said, "You are Christ's body—that's who you are! You must never forget this" (1 Corinthians 12:27, The Message). Without totems to remind you, it is easier than you might think to forget who you are.

> Without totems
> to remind you,
> it is easier than
> you might think
> to forget who
> you are.

Every church is a little culture in itself. Jesus intended these cultures to be distinct, transformational, and even irresistible. Yet as we look across our congregations we often fail to see a transformational culture being birthed from healthy hearts. Instead, we see business as usual. The influence on our churches from the worlds of entertainment, corporate excellence, felt-need marketing, multimedia, technology, and even business management all offer helpful elements, but along the way we need to ask:

- Are our church cultures transforming the broader culture, or mimicking it?
- Are we too susceptible to the latest plug-and-play church program or a pattern of quick fixes?
- Do we care more about doing the next event than about transference of values?
- Will we one day find ourselves filing our mission statement away in a drawer rather than living it?
- Are we stuck, simply mimicking the best practices from others rather than finding out God's best for our church?

A downhill shift from *being* good to *looking* good can bring about spiritual superficiality. Relevance can quickly become an end in itself. Growth can become the highest measurement of success. Responding to consumer demand can distract us from taking a long view.

You don't make a culture shift simply by working harder at the things you're doing. If you want transformation, you must change who you *are*—how you think and what makes your heart beat. You must make sure the heart stuff comes first.

A transformation of environment happens when church leaders embrace the shift in their heart, model it in their lives, and passionately disciple their congregations to become likewise. If these habits and values are central to everything a church does, a healthy, energetic, secure church culture is unleashed, resulting in a better way to grow your church's future.

> You don't make a culture shift simply by working harder at the things you're doing.

The journey may be triggered after you've grown tired of pursuing the latest, newest program for your church. For a brief moment you feel, "It doesn't get better than this," only to be surprised when you still aren't satisfied later on. You might trace your discontent to nagging doubts about your current value system. "There's got to be a better way," you say.

You ask yourself why you seem to be addicted to the quick fix. Or you ponder why you can't identify the misplaced values that are preventing your present approach from working long-range.

> "I *know* what's right, healthy, and best. I just don't know how to *do* it," you say.

Deep down you know what a life-giving culture should look and feel like. "I *know* what's right, healthy, and best. I just don't know how to *do* it," you say.

IDENTIFYING YOUR CHURCH'S UNIQUE CULTURE

By changing your church's culture, you are releasing your church's future. But the first step in the transformation is to identify your current culture. Doing so defines your starting point.

We've all paid a first-time visit to a mall and needed to study the kiosk placed at the entrance. We found a big arrow with the identifier,

"You are here." Then we placed our finger on the place we wanted to reach, and traced a pathway there.

The following questions for discussion and application are designed to give you fresh and confident perspectives on your "you are here" identity. Please take the time to work them through. Future chapters show how we did similar practices at New Hope O'ahu and Fellowship Bible Church.

Exercise One

What Does Your Church Value Most?

Instructions: Begin by analyzing your church's culture through the eyes of an outsider. Imagine that in the last month people from your community participated in your church's worship services, sat in on church programs, met several core people, and learned a bit of the history of your church. The goal in this first set of questions is to describe your church's invisible cultural "megaphone" as it is perceived by an observer.

1. What values are communicated most strongly when someone approaches your church from the outside?

Example: The nice clean facilities, the helpful greeters that assisted us, and the excellent information materials we received to orient our family to the church clearly communicated that they care about newcomers and know how to do things right.

2. What would an outsider, after sitting through several worship services, say your church values *most?*

Example: This church values bringing people to Christ. Every worship service is heavy on evangelism, the preaching is very seeker-oriented, and an invitation to receive Christ into one's life is given every week.

3. What are outsiders' two or three leading perceptions of your church, after they have participated for a month in a variety of your church's programs and ministries?

Example: The leadership is older here. They probably like things just the way they are. They also promise that you will find deep community here, but we have found as newcomers that it is hard to break into this church and develop meaningful friendships.

4. How would an outsider describe the spirit (or attitudes) most prevalent at your church?

5. Read over your impressions, and sum them up. List a handful of values that the church *seems* to be broadcasting. How surprised are you by how they compare to what you want to be known for?

6. Sketch a totem pole that reflects the values you observed. Is this the totem pole you want for your church?

Exercise Two

Test Your Impressions of Another Church

Instructions: If exercise one was difficult for you, you may want to practice by doing the same for a church that is not your own. Doing this exercise may make it easier for you to identify your own church's values afterward.

Exercise Three

Bring in a Focus Group

Instructions: This exercise takes time and effort but pays rich dividends. Put together a small group of people who do not belong to your church but who are willing to look at your church for one month. Afterward, ask them to do exercise one, and then take it a step further by talking to them, perhaps along with other church leaders, about their impressions of your values. How close is their observation to what you *hoped* they would say?

The Four Ingredients

We have found that four ingredients bring a church's culture into focus:

1. *Leadership and values.* What values do members of your church's leadership communicate by their lifestyles? Is it wealth and power? commitment to protecting the status quo? commitment to a cause? modeling of a particular set of behaviors? Leaders more than anyone else set the cultural climate of a church. In many ways, they *are* a church's living totems.

2. *Vision statement.* Is your church's vision something people can identify with and use to measure their spiritual lives? Unfortunately, most vision statements, though well crafted, rarely connect with the everyday lives of church people. A good vision statement is one people can feel and connect with in both an individual and a congregational way.

3. *Symbols, ceremonies, celebrations.* The things you honor, remember, and cheer for are the things you most value. Take a look around your church facilities. What do the symbols say is important? Think back over the last year. Who or what did you honor and celebrate? Who did your church see as its heroes, and why? What got people talking and excited? Embedded in each of these things are your real values.

4. *You as leader.* Ask yourself, "What do I want to accomplish here at this church? What is it that makes me come alive and feel successful before God?" As a leader, you consciously or unconsciously pull everything you do toward the things you really value. That's why it's so important that you be honest about what your values are and how they fit into the values of the church you help to lead.

Mixed together, these ingredients produce the culture of a church. If there is commonality, they not only mix well but reinforce one another. The result is an even stronger overall influence of clarity and power. On the other hand, if these elements clash with one another in some way, the result is confusion, conflict, and a repelling influence that undermines clarity and power.

The next exercise asks you to take a close look at all of these elements and do some thinking about them.

Analyzing Your Church's Current Culture

Instructions: Consider each of these ingredients carefully, and write your assessment of it. Hold on to your responses; we'll use them later.

1. Look at leadership and values.

• Who are the culture setters in your church? (Are they the elected or appointed leaders, or are there unelected leaders who shape the church culture more? Who is *the* leader in setting the culture here at this church?) In your church, one or two leaders may dominate everyone else. Is there a prominent family or persons in the church who control the pastor even though they may not be in a formal leadership position? Do your leadership team members energize one another with the common values they hold, or do they assert conflicting interests?

• What are the primary values exhibited by those who lead here (the senior pastor, the board, unelected but influential leaders in the church)?

• What are the real values coming from each major leadership group? How much unity exists between these groups? In what ways do they clash?

Example: Several long-term board members and their families are keeping the church the way it has always been. They value an "as is" culture and are holding the church back with their influence.

2. Look at the vision statement of your church.

• Is your vision expressed in a serious written document that leaders and the congregation know and embrace?

• Does your vision statement communicate what you really believe and live?

• If it does, what are the cultural values it clearly spells out? If not, where are the gaps?

• If you don't have a written statement, what is the implied or assumed vision?

Write your assessment of your vision statement, and how you are or aren't living it out.

3. Look at your symbols, ceremonies, and celebrations.

• What symbols do you see when you look around your church facility? What do these things say about what you really value? What do they communicate about your culture?

• What ceremonies and rituals does your church honor? How popular are they with the congregation?

• Who are the heroes in your church—the members who are most celebrated, honored, and emulated? What cultural values do those heroes represent?

Write your assessment.

Example: We honor people with strong teaching gifts and people who are generous givers. They get most of the attention at our church.

4. Look at yourself as a leader.

• What do I really value? (Ruthless honesty is required here.)
• What am I really trying to do and build here at this church?
• Is it my passion to build a kingdom culture that honors and serves God, or a culture that rewards me?
• What are my measurements of success as a leader? Do they match up with what I say my real values are?

BOIL IT DOWN

Now it's time to boil down all the observations you've written in this chapter and draw a conclusion. Be as specific as possible.

You might decide, for example, that "A few power players drive our culture. It's a programming-based culture that draws people who primarily want to be entertained." Or you might be even blunter: "Our culture lacks kingdom values. Our values are nothing more than traditions which we follow because they're comfortable and familiar." Maybe your conclusion is a metaphor: "We're like a country club where our primary accomplishments are to take care of each other." Maybe your conclusion is a self-confession: "I don't know what I'm excited about. I used to have spiritual passion, but I've pretty much lost it." Or maybe you will see how your church has untapped potential and energy resting just beneath the surface, waiting to be released.

Exercise Five

The Bottom Line

Instructions: Answer the following questions with some short, highly descriptive phrases.

1. How would I describe our church's current culture?

Example: A mile wide and an inch deep . . . we do children's ministry really well . . . no real discipleship . . . we value creativity . . . we feel more like a country club than a church . . . we care deeply about our church's role in this neighborhood . . . we don't put much emphasis on life transformation . . . many of our leaders live out what they believe . . . we draw people to listen but we don't equip them well . . . our leaders are willing to make courageous changes to reach our community . . . we have competing values that create division and competition . . . we welcome a wide variety of musical styles . . . we're inwardly focused . . . our leadership works hard to give laypeople ownership of ministry . . . we're not bothered by the fact that we're growing older as a congregation . . . newcomers generally have a positive first impression of us . . . our community does "quality" far better than we do . . . our leaders are willing to admit when they're wrong . . . we don't really know what we believe doctrinally . . . we're known as a joyful congregation . . . we have no clear vision or direction for what we're to accomplish . . . we do a good job of honoring our seniors . . . our church is trapped back in the twentieth century . . . our church's environment is one of honesty and authenticity . . . we're afraid of change. . . .

2. Now it's time to boil it down. As I look over the list I just made, what two or three phrases stand out as the key values that presently *drive* the culture of our church? Are these the values I am passionate about and the ones our leadership team believes that God wants for our church?

CAN YOU WRAP YOUR ARMS AROUND IT YET?

By now you should have a pretty good idea of what message your church's culture is sending to your members and to others who come in contact with it. Culture is as real as a profit-and-loss statement. These shared beliefs and values guide behavior, influencing how people think, act, and feel about themselves and each other. If it's a healthy culture, it is almost irresistible!

A healthy culture is almost irresistible.

CHAPTER 5

How to Shift Your Church's Culture

WHEN WE TALK ABOUT MAKING A CULTURE SHIFT, we are talking about changing the default. To take an example, on most computers the default font size is 12 point. If you prefer generally to read print that's a little larger, say 14 point, then you have to permanently modify the default setting. If you change it just for the document you're working on now, then the next time you use the computer, bling! It's back to 12 point again.

Culture shift is a lot like that. You try to instill a new program in your church, and you think you've succeeded, and then the next week—bling!—everything has reverted to the way it was. If this happens week after week after week, you have not really shifted the culture at all. You need to find the cultural default—which is what we worked on in the previous chapter—and reset it by doing hard work that involves not just you but other church leaders, and ultimately everyone in the congregation. Over a period of time, this culture shift occurs, and a new day will dawn.

LEADING THE SHIFT

As a leader in your church, you have the privilege, along with other leaders, of shifting your congregation's culture. If you assess that the culture isn't healthy, you have not only the privilege but the responsibility to shift it. The process of making the shift is not optional; it represents the process of incarnating the kingdom of God.

Jesus made a distinction between people of the kingdom and those who, like the Pharisees, merely hang around the periphery. The Pharisees went to church, prayed, and read the Bible, but Jesus said they had completely missed God's kingdom. He said, "Unless your righteousness surpasses that of the Scribes and Pharisees, you will never enter the kingdom of God" (Matthew 5:20). Jesus also warned, "Not everyone who says to me, 'Lord, Lord,' will enter the kingdom of heaven . . ." (Matthew 7:21).

> A culture shift represents the process of incarnating the kingdom of God.

You can have the right religious words. Your personal Bible may be underlined from cover to cover. You can spend your whole lifetime doing church activities. You can even be an official church leader. Yet with all these good things, you could miss the kingdom of God. You could think that what you're doing is for the kingdom, but it might not be so.

What is God's kingdom? It is the point at which you come under the rule and reign of God. It's where you trade the treasures of this world and an attitude of looking out for yourself in exchange for the treasures and priorities of God.

> Kingdom values cause a church to become more authentic. Genuine life transformation is an inevitable by-product.

But you have to make the choice for kingdom values. Doing so changes the quality of environment that you create. It causes your church to become more authentic and unique, less dependent on someone else's programs, and less likely to duplicate what everyone else is doing. Through a model of incarnation and organic development, kingdom growth marked by genuine life transformation is an inevitable by-product.

You can't steal second base with your foot still on first. We all need to make a choice. Otherwise, we're no better than the Pharisees who looked, acted, and even smelled like kingdom people (even when they weren't kingdom people).

It can't be "your" church if it's going to be God's culture.

A Culture Shift *of* Biblical Proportion

We're not asking you to do something new and untried. Shifting spiritual culture is as old as the nation of Israel. Indeed, Israel's story of movement from the wilderness to settlement of the Promised Land presents a timeless outline for any church or leadership team in how to move a culture from growth-at-any-price to kingdom vision and kingdom reality—from maintenance to health.

> The story of Israel's movement to the Promised Land presents a timeless example of how to move from maintenance to health.

Belief in a Promise

For Israel, and for any spiritual community thereafter, culture shift starts with God's promise. It's the certain hope that spiritual compromise and wilderness wanderings no longer have to be the norm. It's the assurance that things can be better and will be better because God can make it so. But this promise of a new culture must be believed and followed, just as God explained to Israel: "I have set before you today life and prosperity [the promise] . . . in that I command you today to love the Lord your God, to walk in His ways and to keep His commandments and His statutes and His judgments, that you may live and multiply . . ." (Deuteronomy 30:15–16).

We believe this promise still exists today for leaders courageous enough to embrace it for their congregation, regardless of present circumstances.

Leadership That Embraces Kingdom Values

A transition in culture requires fresh leadership. In Israel's case, this meant a new leader whose life and values exemplified a new culture that was about to be constructed. Numbers 27:15–18 puts it this way: "Then Moses spoke to the LORD, saying, 'May the Lord, the God of the spirits of all flesh, appoint a man over the congregation, who will go out and come in before them, and who will lead them out and bring them in, so that the congregation of the Lord will not be like sheep which have no shepherd.' So the Lord said to Moses, 'Take Joshua the son of Nun, a man in whom is the Spirit, and lay your hand on him.'"

Whether your situation requires new leaders is a question you must answer. But in every case, shifting a culture requires a fresh approach from leadership (whether the existing leadership or new).

Broad Support of Kingdom Culture

The transition requires a broad congregational commitment. The congregation must be informed and challenged, and the specifics of the change must be spelled out in detail. This may take time and patience, but in the long run it pays great dividends. The church's leadership must clarify and openly challenge the congregation with this new direction.

Joshua, the successor to Moses, does just this. He brings the people of Israel on board with this new vision of promise. As he does so, he seeks their full commitment. In response, "They answered Joshua, saying, 'All that you have commanded us we will do, and wherever you send us we will go. . . . Only may the Lord your God be with you as He was with Moses'" (Joshua 1:16–17).

Successful Establishment of a Kingdom Culture

Once everyone is on board, you can do the work of setting up a new culture. In Israel's case, this meant war with opposing cultures and weeding out those like Achan (Joshua 7), who were a cancer on this new culture. In the case of a local church transitioning its culture, it may feel like war from time to time. The early days, in particular, have challenges and challengers. But with resolute commitment by a united leadership, perseverance, and most important a close partnership with God, in the end the land is settled, peace returns, and a new culture is established.

> With firm commitment to God's promise, Israel left the wilderness and eventually shifted the culture of Palestine.

If making such a journey seems overwhelming to you, imagine what it felt like to Joshua. To succeed, the answer to the question "Is it worth it?" must be "Yes: I desire a rich culture where an authentic spiritual community lives out kingdom values in powerful ways in partnership with the living God." More important, how much *less* than that standard is acceptable to you? If you are still trying to convince yourself that you can solve a culture problem with a series of patchwork quick fixes; be warned, such an approach always fails.

Israel did not remain in the wilderness. The young country experienced resistance and obstacles, but its leaders believed that God had promised them a land. With firm commitment to that promise, Israel left the wilderness and eventually shifted the culture of Palestine.

You can too.

WILL YOU BE *a* PRESENT-DAY JOSHUA?

Like Joshua (or Joshua's leadership team), you've got to believe that God has promised you a land. You may wrestle with traditions, structure, staff, and board. But kingdom values can help bring them around, and a unifying culture will result. Eventually it will release its potential. There is hope. Believe it.

We have met many present-day Joshuas. One of them was appointed to lead a mainline, denominational church with deep-set traditions. He quickly found himself mired in a church culture that was going nowhere.

Yes, this congregation loved his wonderful preaching, his helpful teaching, and the strong pastoral attention he gave them. But, no, they did not embody a healthy spiritual culture. Their forms no longer fit, a number of their lifestyles were compromised, and their focus of attention was inward. Worse, they liked it that way.

Our friend, however, could not rest in this wilderness. Bravely, he chose to believe that God would use him to shift this ineffective culture.

He began on two fronts. On the one side, he took the time to pray and think through the kingdom values he believed should make up this new culture. He made a personal commitment to authentically embrace them and live them out. At the same time, he wisely built strong relationships with his people without disturbing the status quo at the time. In this way, he not only began to understand in detail the present culture of the congregation and how it had come about but also built good relationships with them and earned their trust.

Over two years, he slowly replaced or converted much of the existing leadership to this new kingdom vision, again while maintaining the status quo. When new staff was hired, he made sure they embraced these new values.

He also offered a special class to anyone in the church who wanted it. The name was an advertisement in itself: "Envisioning the Church of the Future." The class went on for months, with lots of healthy dialogue. Many emerging leaders participated, as did some established leaders. They discussed ideas, possibilities, and opportunities. He shared with his class the kingdom lifestyle he was passionately pursuing. Many class participants told him they wanted that way of life too.

When the moment was right, he presented to his leadership team the values he was so passionate about. He offered it with a challenge: he voiced it as a new vision for the entire church. He knew the moment was right because a large majority of the leaders now around him had already been won over to these new cultural ideas. Now was the time to "take the land." A few longtime members objected. By this point, though, the leadership majority was for changing not just a few scattered programs but the very culture of the church.

We wish we could tell you everything went smoothly after that. It didn't. When the vision was presented to the whole church, several camps resisted like guardians of tradition. Some even left the church. Others were later won over because of the trust capital our friend had established in the years before the new vision was unleashed, when he simply loved the people just as they were. Some, however, were simply overruled because their previous power plays no longer worked. A few even remain to this day, unconvinced the church did the right thing and taking shots when they can.

But the good news is this: a new culture was successfully birthed at this church under our friend's courageous leadership. He did it! God did it!

Go there today, and you find a congregation that is vibrant and alive. They are reaching out to their community in bold, fresh ways. Their lifestyles exude an authenticity that is contagious and wholesome. The people are of one spiritual mind. Gone are the days when traditions could not be challenged, when great preaching was the only measure of success, or where sin in people's lives was rarely addressed.

It's a new church, born again from inside out.

What You Can Do *to* Shift Your Culture

The book's final chapter opens with a summary progression of how to shift your church's culture. The present section shows the factors that you'll need to consider.

Huddle and Assess the Present

Begin by assessing your present culture. You should use the exercises in Chapter Four to help you bring your present church culture into clear focus.

Assess your attitude toward it. How confident are you that God can grow a kingdom culture through your church? How much faith do you have that he will go before you and actually bring it to pass? Indeed, God will give you favor and bring about victory over every obstacle, but only as you consecrate your life and efforts to building God's kingdom, not your own.

How much spiritual potential do you see in your church? You need to acknowledge that regardless of how your congregation looks now, it has the potential of spiritual billionaires. This potential is already present in the people of your congregation and those they are reaching. How you develop the people of your church is directly related to how you think about and view them.

Which other leaders or board members stand with you in modeling and advocating a kingdom vision? Identify where God is already at work through your people. Continue to cooperate with God's anointing.

Who are the key people who hinder kingdom culture at your church? How do they express their influence? How will you handle those who defy this new kingdom vision? Do you ignore it or confront it? If the latter, how do you handle confrontation?

Ask what is opening doors right now. What draws newcomers? What kind of encounters with God are people finding most irresistible? Your answer helps you identify the real totems in your church's present culture.

What kind of babies does your nursery cultivate? Where do future leaders thrive most?

Identify unhealthy, outside-in aspects of your current culture, such as an addiction to the quick fix or a pattern of cloning someone else's plug-and-play program. Identify where you're missing the mark, or perhaps even treating the wrong thing.

Which present approaches are helping to grow your culture into the inheritance God wants to provide?

Assess Your Role in Shaping the Future

As a leader of the church, do you embrace and passionately live out a kingdom vision? Remember, it must first flow out of you before it will convince anyone else. It must be a godly vision, not a vision of "how to become a big church" or "how to be the star around here." Leaders must search their hearts first before they can shift the culture.

What do *you* believe God wants your church to be known for? What kind of culture must this church embrace if it is to be a kingdom culture?

Be willing to make personal changes in how you think and what makes your heart beat. Embrace the desired culture in your heart, making sure the heart stuff comes first. This affects your personal devotional life, and it may require repentance. It starts with you, the leader, acknowledging that your key role is to be the tutor who cultivates a culture that releases this potential into the lives of your people.

Do self-examination for what you love most about the potential in your church. Most likely, whatever you love and brag about is the kind of culture you're already developing. As a leader, you carry the culture in yourself.

Check your life for inconsistencies in what you model. How would an observer assess the difference between your statements about "That's what we want tomorrow" and the actual fruit you're producing? The environment shaping your actual fruit *is* your actual culture.

List and Enlist

List the concrete values that would exemplify the preferred culture. Are they biblical? Are they positive? This is important to do because they will ultimately lead to your totems. Enlist buy-in from other leaders. Talk and teach them. Encourage healthy dialogue and discussion.

In short, convert others, particularly the leadership team around you, to embrace the same values you do. Be patient. This takes time. But your goal is to have a majority of your board and staff embrace these new values with you before you go further.

Expect God to go before you in this. Watch God fight your battles and win over your opponents.

Set your sights on following an incarnational path to grow a healthy, God-honoring culture.

With other leaders on board, begin communicating the vision to others. Stop focusing on what is; focus instead on what the kingdom vision for your church should be. George Barna's definition of vision is "a clear mental image of a preferable future imparted by God" to a willing servant.[1]

Always keep in mind that a kingdom vision should be primarily an organic vision of what to be. "What to do" visions come and go. A "what to be" vision is one that never changes.

Identify how your church is learning to steward its inheritance in Christ. How are you currently growing your culture into the inheritance God wants to provide? How are you now creating space for people to grow?

Write and Display

Write down the new kingdom vision in specific *be* language. Remember that Jesus started with a *be* vision (the Beatitudes, Matthew 5:3–11) for his church. So should we, by asking, "What are we going to be?"

As a leadership team, adopt a kingdom vision of *being* as your church's vision statement. Put it in writing. Years ago at Fellowship, our elders adopted a mission statement that reads in part, "To equip Christians to be . . . passionately committed to Jesus Christ, morally pure, biblically measured, family centered, financially faithful, evangelistically bold, and socially responsible." That's our *be* vision.

Make it your goal to have every leader passionately behind your new kingdom vision. One key to a healthy church culture is leadership unified around a vision. A chorus is always better than a solo in setting culture.

> A chorus is always better than a solo in setting culture.

Live and Teach

Begin the process of filtering this leadership-embraced kingdom vision into the life and programs of the church. Walk your church through your totems, from the pulpit in a sermon series. (It's good to do so in some way every year.) Display this vision in key and appropriate places. Discuss the vision in small groups or Sunday school classes with some of your elders or other leaders present for dialogue.

Use your kingdom vision when you hire staff, disciple new believers, generate new ideas, measure the success of events and programming, select new leaders, and so on. It should be communicated to the congregation often, in both written materials and real-life stories.

> Be a life-giving church filled with Spirit-led people who minister from life in the Son and pursue their heavenly Father's calling.

Note that the filtering process takes time. Shifting culture takes time.

Passionately disciple your congregation to become a life-giving church filled with Spirit-led people who minister from the energy of their life in the Son, who have been released and encouraged to pursue what their heavenly Father has called them to do.

Keep your focus on releasing people, understanding that you release culture through people. Spiritually energized people *are* the convincing point in a culturally healthy congregation.

Celebrate and Honor

If your values are centered on life transformation, then who in your church looks like that? Feature them in church services or sermon illustrations. Let them tell their story through testimony. Make video clips to profile them. Give awards or host parties for those who exemplify and embody what the church is all about.

Whatever you show off and sing praises about, people will want to imitate or be part of. After identifying heroes, make a big deal of whatever ministry they're doing. Be a recruiter for *their* ministry. Come to *their* events when they invite you. In general, as you go to serve them, others catch on that this is the kind of ministry you hope to see more of.

Keep the emphasis on serving the body, and never make yourself the hero.

Anticipate in faith that once these habits and values are central to everything a church does, a healthy, energetic, secure church culture is unleashed, resulting in a far better way to grow your church's future.

Check and Recheck

How are you being held accountable? Who is holding you accountable? How does correction happen if you deviate from a kingdom-focused vision? For example, at Fellowship we do an annual review of our values as an elder board in a yearly retreat setting. We also present this review and our accountability to our values to the congregation in an annual "state of the church" message.

Exercise Six

Measuring the Transition

As you shift your culture, the best way to begin measuring your transition is to take stock of where you are now. Use the checklist in this exercise as a starting point, and hang onto it. Come back to it in a year or so to check the progress of your church's culture shift. Once your church has turned the corner and is becoming an irresistible culture (as described in the final chapter of this book), your description of the "now" will be quite different from what it is today.

Instructions: Think about how close your church is to a model of healthy kingdom living. Using the Now column, rate your church on a scale from 1 (low) to 10 (high).

As you rate each item, ask yourself, "What is the most strategic action we can take to improve in this area?" Write the action.

Category	NOW _____ (today's date)		FUTURE _____ (a year or two later)	
	Rating 1–10	Improvement to Make	Rating 1–10	Improvement to Make
1. Clarity as a leader about what our kingdom values should be				
2. Unity among our leaders on what our new vision is				
3. A specific "be" mission statement				
4. Staff understanding and acceptance				
5. Congregational buy-in				
6. Ministry adjustments that reflect the new kingdom vision				
7. Yearly accountability and evaluation of progress				
8. Other:				
9. Other:				
10. Other:				

Here are some critical questions you might be asking at this point:

• *How can I get my board to agree that we need a culture shift? Mine is so difficult to work with that I don't know where to start.*

Involve the board in getting input. If they do some hard, objective scouting (interviews, survey, focus groups, and so on), they will experience the issues firsthand. If you say, "Here's what's going on," the board members can object if they're out of touch, but if they discover it for themselves they are more likely to agree that a shift is needed.

Remember too that, deep inside, most board members genuinely want God's best for the church. Many will respond positively if you paint a preferred future of what could and should be the culture of the church. Don't pitch it so much as "what I want the church to become" but rather as a God-honoring, biblical, forward movement that's compelling.

• *How can I present this idea to my congregation without overwhelming them?*

Prayerfully assess how much they can absorb and process, and then roll out the shift in manageable stages. New pastors especially tend to see lots of changes needed, but if they're not careful they may run the ship on the rocks because they haven't yet built up enough trust capital.

You might begin by telling people what will *not* change. For example, "What will never change around here is God's original call for us to do service for others." Part of the leader's responsibility is to restore a church back to God's intent. You don't want to make the sheep skittish! Most people are reticent about change; instead of thinking out of the box they're more comfortable returning to God—who made the box! If they can feel as if they're going back to their roots, they'll make great strides forward.

• *Does the responsibility for determining the specifics of the culture shift rest solely on me as a leader and what I think God is telling me?*

Yes and no. A culture shift cannot happen unless the main leaders of the church want to embrace kingdom values from the heart. It also won't happen without widespread ownership among all the church's leaders as they polish and confirm the vision.

At the same time, it's important to remember that change begins in many places. Some change is leader-initiated, or it can move up from the grassroots. The leader's job is to be open to the truth, wherever it comes from.

A caveat: learn to detect the difference between reformers and rebels. When leaders sense a rebellion, they tend to get defensive; be sure you are not mistaking a reformer for a rebel. Real reformers have the church's best interest in mind, and they convey a spirit of give and take.

• *What is the most important thing to remember when making a culture shift?*

Always keep in mind that good shepherds don't beat their sheep. It's better to lead and persuade people than to drive them. Young church leaders can be so fervent about moving a church to pure kingdom values that they relentlessly *drive* people rather than leading them. Slow down. Modeling and persuasion generally work better than browbeating.

Avoid an approach of "me versus you" or "us versus them." Change always raises the issue of who has the most authority. Don't go that way. Preach for agreement—not "*Who's* right?" but "*What's* right?" You would like everyone who wants God's best for their church to say, "Yes, we need to be that" and "Yes, we've got to do that."

• *How much time does a culture shift take? How will I know how fast to move?*

There is no set timeline that's the same for everyone. Every church is different. Some are more deeply set in unhealthy practices, while others are already headed in a new direction. Every church has an optimum rate of growth, depending on its age, maturity, denominational ties, and other factors. Just as you wouldn't drive an old Volkswagen as fast as you would a new Ferrari, you must evaluate and grasp the right speed of change for your church.

Finally, don't make the mistake of thinking that a culture shift is occurring just because everyone is agreeing with the vision. The true test is when you can see the change implemented in people's lives.

Divine Partnership

WHO DO YOU THINK IS BETTER AT BUILDING A church, you or the Holy Spirit? Who is better at shifting a church's culture, you or the Holy Spirit? We all know the obvious answers, but we don't always understand practically how the partnership is supposed to work.

At one of New Hope's conferences, a pastor who spoke with me was feeling great pressure to find a new program and get it launched quickly. I reminded him that leading ministry isn't about a fast fix or a continuous sequence of imported programs. "It's all about developing a culture, and letting the Holy Spirit do the work through you," I explained.

"That sounds so much better," the pastor replied. I could see the sense of release in his face. "So our first responsibility is to position ourselves to welcome and cooperate with the work of the Holy Spirit," he observed.

> The ultimate culture shifter is the Holy Spirit.

He is right. We furnish the atmosphere and platform, and the Holy Spirit is faithful to be the teacher, motivator, challenger, and comforter. After all, the ultimate culture shifter is the Holy Spirit.

HS
lds change

Scripture says that God "gives the Spirit without measure" (John 3:34). Whether we bring a thimble, a bucket, or a barrel, God will fill it. The question is not how much of the Holy Spirit is available, but which container our faith opens for him. If I've got just a thimble's worth of faith, he'll fill it. But if I open my entire heart to faith, he'll fill that too. My job is to hang close to Jesus and open myself wide.

When I was in junior high school in Oregon, our class took a field trip to a huge underground cavern. During the tour, some friends and I decided to stay back and explore on our own. But when the guide left our part of the cave, so did the light. We had a terrible time. It was the darkest place I had ever experienced. We couldn't even see our hands in front of our faces. To make matters worse, we could hear the group getting farther and farther away from us. Scared that we might fall off the narrow walkway at one of the cliff-like junctions, we mostly crawled around on our knees until we found our guide with her light.

Cutting away from the guide was dumb and scary. It was no fun at all, as our bruised and bloody knees affirmed.

Years later, I took the same tour but did it the right way by staying in the light. It was the most beautiful underground sight I had ever seen. Both times I was on the same journey and in the same environment. The only variable was my distance from the guide.

THE SPIRIT *as* YOUR CHURCH'S GUIDE *and* PARTNER

Jesus promises that the Holy Spirit, who knows the future of your church, "will guide you into all the truth" (John 16:13). This means the truth of your church's future needs a guide. Passages such as Luke 24:49 and Acts 1:4–8 can be summarized this way: "You don't know what's coming around the corner, so wait for the Spirit's lead and then follow." As the Holy Spirit's power works within us, God "is able to do far more abundantly beyond all that we ask or think" (Ephesians 3:20).

Your journey is a partnership. Jesus says "follow me" some twenty times in the Gospels. To do so requires that *both* of you must walk. Greg Ogden's book *Transforming Discipleship* observes that there are actually three phases in walking with Jesus as his disciple: "Come and see," "follow me," and finally "come and be with me."[1] As you follow Jesus in that walk, you will be transformed to reflect the "glory of the Lord" (2 Corinthians 3:18).

> Jesus says, "Follow me." To do so requires that *both* of you must walk.

This is what the Holy Spirit does to your church as well. If your congregation abides in relationship to Christ, as John 15:1–11 outlines, the fruit is fruit of the Holy Spirit: "love, joy, peace, patience, kindness, goodness, faithfulness, gentleness, [and] self-control" (Galatians 5:22–23). As God matures our congregations in these qualities, we become more like him individually and corporately. Our greatest inheritance is a likeness to Christ. God manifests Jesus Christ through people; the word *Christian* means "little Christ."

Imagine that a professional baseball player has a young daughter playing Little League. The daughter dreams of hitting home runs like her dad. So the dad teaches his daughter how to stand, how to watch the ball, how to swing, and how to follow through. He imparts his ability by training his child, giving her knowledge of stance, positioning, timing, and the like.

It might be easier for the dad to say, "Here, I'll do it for you." Instead, he limits himself. The father is basically hitting the ball through the child. In a way, the father transfers his character, life, and heart to the daughter. As she listens to her father, something of the father's skill, depth, and confidence is deposited in the girl.

There is one hitch, however. The child must follow her father's instructions if she is to learn to hit those home runs. Obedience and cooperation are required; they're not optional.

God is like that with us. He wants to do his work through us. He tells us to follow, and we will become like him. This is the foundation for working together with the Holy Spirit to shift the culture in your church.

TRUSTING GOD *to* WORK THROUGH OTHERS

The Holy Spirit can be trusted—far more than leaders in most churches allow—to directly extend his work through *all* of God's people, not just through certain designated leaders. The Bible says every believer is a minister. The same Holy Spirit who lives in a church's leadership is the same Holy Spirit who lives in each follower of Jesus Christ.

Following God and becoming like him is the foundation for working together with the Holy Spirit to shift the culture in your church.

God's promise of the Holy Spirit is not just a nice saying or a hopeful expectation. He's a living promise to be the living tutor, a guide along the way, for all who have been "born of the Spirit" (John 3:8).

As pastors, both of us put focus on growing "big" people. That's far more important than a focus on building big-attendance churches. "Big" people know firsthand how to depend on and follow the promptings of the Holy Spirit.

Paul said, "I keep working toward that day when I will finally be all that Christ Jesus saved me for and wants me to be" (Philippians 3:12 NLT).

Paul wanted to be sure he attained the potential God intended for his life and ministry. That's why he stayed close to the Holy Spirit. The same is true for each of Christ's disciples today.

Leaders alone can't complete the mission of the church.

Just think: if every single person in our churches became all God created us to be, the results would be dramatic. We're *all* moving under the power of God.

Leaders alone can't complete the mission of the church. If we train our people to let the plow of the Holy Spirit touch every corner of their hearts and lives, then do we trust them enough to help them find full and direct access to God?

Your church's leadership is the personification of your church's culture—the living totems who influence others by demonstrating what the kingdom of God could look like as expressed through a particular church. But the Holy Spirit, who is at work in *every* believer, wants the rest of the church to become living totems as well.

The breadth of your church depends on how many living totems you can develop and release. Great leaders have a unique ability to create many living totems who live out the values that the leaders have perceived and objectified for the congregation.

Great leaders want to give their people as direct a connection with God as possible. Then as God's people listen to the Spirit, we leaders don't want to stand in their way. Our trust is that when people are engaged in the Spirit's work in their lives, good stuff will happen through the church.

The Holy Spirit
Continues Working After We're Gone

Yet another advantage of partnering with the Holy Spirit is how he continues to work long after we have gone.

Few parents ever forget the moment of dropping off their first child at college. For the first time, their son or daughter is now at the wheel of life alone. After the last hug, the final goodbye, and a few parting words, the parents tearfully head back home. "Well, she's truly on her own now," they say to each other. Or perhaps, "We've given him all we could; we have to trust God now that it will stick." Their concern is whether their child reproduces the culture that they, as parents, have tried to instill for the last eighteen years or so.

Church leaders often go through a similar anxiety. "Are we fostering a ministry culture that will last?" they ask each other, wondering if what they have deposited in the congregation has genuine sticking power.

The answer does not rest on our good intentions alone. As we find out what the "Jesus of our community is doing" (in Dietrich Bonhoeffer's phrasing), our primary responsibility is to make sure everything we do is in partnership with the Holy Spirit. Then, after we're no longer present, he's still there, working away in the minds and hearts of the congregation.

HAMMER *out* YOUR OWN TRUMPET

Numbers 10:1–10 gives instructions for creating a new type of trumpet: long straight metal tubes of silver about three or four feet long, and flaring out at the end. Predictably, each of these hand-crafted trumpets has its own sound. The Lord's instruction to Moses emphasizes the individual quality of each instrument ("of hammered work you shall make them . . ."; Numbers 10:2). The new trumpet was then used to guide God's people forward in worship, ministry, and battle.

The most effective leaders don't buy trumpets off the shelf for their ministry; they craft them from their own lives and understandings. Bill Hybels has a ministry trumpet. It blows well for him because he hammered it out himself. Buying an identical copy of his trumpet probably won't work for your setting. David Yonggi Cho's trumpets won't be exactly right for you either. Nor will Rick Warren's, T. D. Jakes's, Robert Schuller's, Cynthia Hale's, Andy Stanley's, or that of any other pastor you look up to.

Hammering out your own trumpet means asking for the Holy Spirit's wisdom about how best to represent the kingdom of God in your community. Ask God, "What totems do you want this church to proclaim and become?"

If you take the easy road and buy your trumpet at someone else's church conference, cloning their programs and using their materials without appropriate adaptation, you will find the road leading to a dead end. Your trumpet needs to be hammered from your church's own precious metal.

What if you *enjoy* building another church's culture, instead of being the real you? "Lord, I know I'm not hammering out my trumpet; I'm blowing someone else's," you might say. "But it sounds good, and people like it, so why not?" It's a logical question. But the problem is that you'll develop a mutant culture, not the true culture of your own unique church. The Holy Spirit doesn't want you to clone what others are doing; hammer out a trumpet that fits your unique church context.

> The Holy Spirit wants you to hammer out a trumpet that fits your unique church context.

Remember the press hoopla a few years ago about Dolly, the first cloned sheep? Soon, however, came another announcement: "Dolly is dead." She had massive mutations, lung disease, cysts, breakdowns in thyroid, tumors, and more. The cloned sheep was not as strong as the original sheep.

If we're not careful, we can do the same in the body of Christ: become a clone of someone else's program, only to experience major organ failure. At first, plug-and-play seems to be a good answer, but too often it leads to becoming a mutant culture.

> At first, plug-and-play seems to be a good answer, but too often it leads to becoming a mutant culture.

If you don't know who you are, you become like everybody else. The Lord doesn't want us to be like everybody else, never knowing who we really are. He wants us to be contextualized leaders whose words and deeds spring from his Source yet are uniquely ours.

LIVING *by* FAITH, ENTERING *the* UNKNOWN

Have you ever rappelled down a cliff?

Imagine yourself atop a two-hundred-foot bluff in the Rockies, peering over a ledge, preparing to rappel down it, and double-checking that your life support—the rope feeding through your carabiner—is in place. To get to your goal of firm ground, you have to hold onto your rope, lean back, and jump off—backwards!—into the unknown.

Living in the Spirit and leading a culture shift is a lot like rappelling. You have to make some uncomfortable, even radical choices. You don't know what it will feel like at each point in the transition, but you're confident your life support (the Holy Spirit) will be with you every moment. One voice inside you says, "This is nuts. Go back to patterns you already know." But you hear the voices of those who have gone ahead of you, a chorus led by the Holy Spirit. They affirm that you're about to experience a dimension of life that ultimately you will never want to replace.

Rappelling down a cliff has three stages. First is the fear of the unknown before you jump. Next come some breathtaking thrills on the way down. Then, when you land, you feel deep satisfaction.

The same thing happens when you walk (or jump) with the Spirit into places previously unknown to you. You know by faith what's there, but you can't see it. Nor can you access it until you actually jump. It requires all your courage to put fear aside and take a leap of faith. But after you do, you have incredibly deep satisfaction. You know that what you did has brought your church closer to the kingdom of God. "No church-of-the-year award, new worship facility, or other temporary boost can match this!" you conclude.

> If you're in Christ, the Holy Spirit is alive in you, and nothing is more thrilling than partnering with him.

The good news is that if you're in Christ, the Holy Spirit is alive in you, and nothing is more thrilling than partnering with him. Inside your heart, soul, and spirit is the living God, wanting to move in you and your congregation, and helping you know you're part of a movement that's eternal and true.

This joy is one of the many fruits of developing a new culture for your church.

PERSONAL HOPE, CORPORATE HOPE

Living in the same section of Little Rock, pastoring the same congregation, and attending the same Razorback football games—all for more than twenty years—has enabled people to size me up pretty well. They've seen areas where I've grown, and many of them know an area of weakness for me that's just under the surface of my personality: anger.

It's because I grew up in an angry family. Most of my childhood recollections are of my parents screaming at each other ("You failed in this!" and "Get off my back!"). As my brothers and I grew up, we followed suit. We solved problems not by talking but by knocking a hole in the wall. My brothers once locked me out of the house, and to get back inside I tore the door off the hinges and kicked it in. We cussed at each other, and people were afraid of us. That's what I learned for eighteen years. That was my long-established culture.

Whatever progress I've made, I owe to one source: my Savior. God forgave my sins through Jesus back in 1968, and the Holy Spirit has been working a transformation from the inside out ever since. With God's help, I chose not to let anger steal my life. I decided to find the root that caused my anger and change whatever behaviors fueled it. I enlisted others to help me change. In doing so, my long-established culture of anger by the grace of God eventually transitioned into one better marked by a culture of Christlikeness.

> Whatever culture is in your church now, it can be transformed into a culture like unto the kingdom of God.

When I look back and see how the Spirit has worked personally, resulting in a dramatic then-and-now difference, it's only a short hop for me to believe that God can do the same things in the culture of a church. I'm convinced that regardless of whatever culture is in your church now, it can likewise be transformed into a culture like unto the kingdom of God. Such is the privilege of partnering with the Holy Spirit. He is the ultimate culture shifter.

Exercise Seven

Discerning the Holy Spirit

Instructions: The Book of Acts (often nicknamed "Acts of the Holy Spirit") mentions more than fifty times how the Holy Spirit works through the church. In Acts 15:28 the apostles explained a decision they made by saying, "It seemed good to the Holy Spirit and to us."

In this exercise, take the opportunity to make some observations about how you discern the same level of Holy Spirit partnership at your church today.

1. Think about an important leadership decision you recently made. On a scale of 1 (low) to 10 (high), how strongly did you sense the leading of the Spirit?

2. This chapter opened with a pastor who was advised, "It's all about developing a culture, and letting the Holy Spirit do the work through you." How do you relate to the story? How are you learning to partner with the Holy Spirit? Be specific.

3. Think about a decision your church needs to make in the near future. How can this decision be made in greater partnership with the Holy Spirit? What is your part?

Growing the Culture at New Hope O'ahu

THE STORY IS TOLD OF A WEALTHY AND arrogant businessman who arranged to be part of an African safari but arrived three days late. He hired some locals and set out immediately, pushing them hard. "Keep moving quickly; we need to catch up," he cried, with no regard for the strain he was putting on them.

The next morning he ran around impatiently, summoning, "Everyone up!" He fumed at the team leader, "Hurry up, get your men going." By day's end, all the porters had collapsed in exhaustion. The next morning he goaded everyone to rise promptly, and then he pressed them all day. That night they collapsed again. On the fourth morning, no one moved, so he started blowing his whistle. "I'm paying you good money," he said to the team leader, "so get your men going."

The team leader looked him in the eye and replied, "My men will not move all day. You've been pushing us so hard the last three days that we need a whole day to let our souls catch up with us!"

Fast-paced, driven Christian leaders, even those with the best of intentions, often feel like members of this tired team: they are running as fast as they can, but somewhere along the way they left their soul behind. They feel lost—for good reason.

God is not cracking the whip; he is waiting patiently for us. We too may need time before God to let our souls catch up. Otherwise we'll do ministry without soul—and too many of us are skilled enough to do just that. If we maintain and manage by rote, the church's culture doesn't develop healthily. It's like running on a treadmill: we expend great energy but our ministry doesn't get anywhere.

Our soul grows weary before our feet do. As soon as we lose heart, we're moving too fast. It takes heart to cooperate with the Holy Spirit.

• • • • •

Now that you know what's involved in shifting the culture at your church, we'll let you in on a secret: It's not always easy. In this section and the next, we share our own stories in some detail. We hope our experiences will help you with yours.

Part Three shows how Wayne and New Hope O'ahu chose a simpler culture with a lot of heart rather than becoming complex at the cost of their souls.

Identifying New Hope's Totems

S OME YEARS AGO, MY WIFE, ANNA, AND I WENT TO
Nashville, Tennessee, where I was to speak at a church. As we
walked outside the airport, the hot summer sun hit me so hard I
thought my eyebrows would singe. We wondered how plants, let alone
humans, could endure the heat of the brutal, dry Tennessee summer.
It was quite a contrast with the delightful Hawaiian weather we had
just left.

Then we entered our hotel, and it was like stepping into a whole
new world. The five-acre, climate-controlled hotel was amazing. We
found ourselves in a cool, soothing, environment with a waterfall, a
stream, and a huge botanical garden—all indoors. We saw plant spe-
cies from Hawaii. They were growing like
weeds here because the conditions were just
right. Vegetation that would have died outside in five minutes was fruitful and blos-
soming on the inside.

"This is a picture of the church!" I ex-
claimed to Anna. People whose lives are bar-
ren, dying, and shriveling can come into the
embrace of the church and thrive. Those
who need fertile soil for their lives will find

> People whose lives
> are barren, dying,
> and shriveling
> can come into the
> embrace of the
> church and thrive.

help here. They can be fruitful because of the good growing environment. "This island of health is like the kingdom of God," we agreed.

No matter what its geography, a church can condition the environment to cultivate a culture of fruitfulness in which those who join with them can thrive, much like the "hundred-fold" harvest that Jesus describes in Mark 4:3–8, 13–20. The secret according to Jesus is to cultivate the soil. Each section of his parable has a similar beginning: same seed, same farmer, and same soil. The difference shows up in the conditions around the soil.

Rocky soil, for example, has shale underneath. It warms the soil and helps germinate the seed quickly, but the plant soon withers since the roots can't penetrate the hard rock to reach the cool water below. In fair weather, the people of a rocky-soil church might seem fine, but when things around them heat up—maybe a little complaining here, a little rebellion there—they lose heart and want to resign. They wither.

Fruitful soil, in contrast, produces a rich harvest. Likewise people who are guided into fertile environments tend to grow in healthy ways.

CULTIVATING FERTILE SOIL

Fortunately, we are not stuck with the soil we begin with. We can condition the soil of even the rockiest church so that it will bring the greatest fruitfulness.

All agrarian societies understand the value of cultivation. Farmers today can tell you about certain highly valued practices: plowing, hoeing, fertilizing, and watering. They can show you their tools. They might even have a town square with a display that represents the qualities their community values—a statue of a farmer tilling the soil, family members planting seeds, a bountiful harvest—the fruits of the fertile soil they have worked so hard to cultivate. Everyone in the community sees this display, every day, and understands it to say, "This is what we do;

> We can condition the soil of even the rockiest church so that it will bring the greatest fruitfulness.

this is who we are." Any stranger walking into town knows all about the heart of the people who live here.

Sound familiar? That's right: we're talking about totems again.

In ancient Israel, God had Moses tell the Israelites to "make for themselves tassels on the corners of their garments." When they see the tassels, they will "remember all the commandments of the LORD," walking with God so as to "be holy" (Numbers 15:38–40). The tassels were reminders or symbols that would represent principles, or characteristics that identified them as a nation of God-fearing people.

These tassels can be found throughout the annals of history, characterizing tribes, families, and even nations. For example, if you had lived in the Europe of yesteryear, your family would have a coat of arms. Each symbol would represent something. Maybe you'd say, "Our family crest shows that we were blacksmiths and were strong."

In some areas of Japan, villages display huge stones called obelisks with their village ideals written on them. A stone might read "Patience, Peace, and Endurance." In Alaska, most of the Native American totem polls are animals that represent skills and values the tribe needs. The totem pole announces to everyone, "This is our culture." From generation to generation, village elders model and teach how people should live out those values in their daily lives. In cultivating the soil of community life, they deposit these values into the next generation.

CHURCH TOTEMS

What are some of the totems we're building into the culture of New Hope Christian Fellowship O'ahu? Our symbols are prominently displayed, just like a totem pole in the village square.

When you enter our ministry center, you can't miss a display of our mission statement; it highlights evangelism, discipleship, equipping, and extension. As you walk through the hallways, you see our core values listed on another wall, along with posters of people in relationship. They remind us that everything we do is about people: you, your sister, your brother, your parents, your children, your friends, and other relationships that are special to you. On one wall you see a big sign: "Doing Church as a Team." In one person's office you see a sling with five smooth stones, designed to remind the person that "I can do all things through Him who strengthens me" (1 Samuel 17:40; Philippians 4:13). These symbolic totems help us remember and live out all of God's commandments.

If we don't live out our values, then we won't pass them on.

But of course, it is not enough simply to state or symbolize what we believe. We can have great slogans, and even glossy printed literature, but if we don't live out our values, then we won't pass them on. A healthy church culture is built in tandem with understood totems that are biblical and eternal, but it is also modeled by leaders who express these totems in their daily lives.

Let's take a closer look at how some of our totems are lived out by the people of the New Hope community.

Evangelism

Everything we do at New Hope is tied to a soul. The word *evangelism* represents the heart we have for people who are lost, whose relationship with God has been broken.

More than ten thousand people worship each weekend in our eight locations on O'ahu (they cover a forty-mile spread). All nineteen services are held in rented property, requiring a weekly routine of setting everything up and taking it back down. At two of our locations, the first Sunday morning service is currently at 7:00 A.M., so it is not unusual for set-up team members to rise at 3:00 A.M. and be unloading equipment vans before sunrise.

Sometimes I drop by to encourage these hard-working servants. "I'm setting up a speaker column," someone may explain to me on being asked.

"No you're not," I reply. "It may look like you're connecting a wire, but you're doing the work of an evangelist. You're preparing the

CV

place so someone can hear the gospel, and it will be possible only because the sound system is connected and positioned just right."

I'm not exaggerating. When someone prays along with me to receive Christ at the close of the service, it isn't just the pastor who gets the message through. The man, woman, or teen who sets up the sound system makes it possible for others not to miss what God wants to say to them through the message.

Sometimes I'll ask someone who is having a rough morning in our nursery with a cranky child, "What are you doing?" I want this person to see a connection to evangelism. The volunteer's labor of love that morning is accomplishing even more than offering Christlike care to a child. It's also a gift to the child's single mother, making it possible for her to stay focused on the worship and message, knowing that her precious one is in caring, capable hands.

As I write this chapter, we are rejoicing that last week 185 people indicated they have entered a relationship with Jesus Christ, inviting him into their lives. In the same week, we baptized 158 other people, as outward testimony that they now want to be publicly identified with Jesus Christ.

It takes a whole church of evangelists for these life transformations to happen.

Developing Emerging Leaders

Early in my years as a guitar player, my teachers told me I should know the songs so well that they become second nature, something almost intuitive. I should be able to play a song on my guitar while I'm fully engaged in watching a television program.

I took the challenge literally and eventually learned how to play "Dixie" on the high strings and "Yankee Doodle" on the bottom strings while singing "Old McDonald Had a Farm"—all simultaneously. It worked! I learned that a guitarist can play without having to think about the mechanical part of which finger goes where. The memorized finger work freed me to focus on something else, such as singing "Old McDonald" at the same time.

The same principle works in anyone preparing to do spiritual ministry. Leaders need to practice until what they've consciously learned becomes second nature. They don't want to be like the musician who painstakingly shifts fingers from one chord to the next, hoping the sounds come out right but unable to think beyond that level.

In ministry, we need to be so familiar with our tools (starting with our most basic one, the Bible) that we're like someone sitting atop a bottomless well, effortlessly able to scoop up more and more refreshing water. At that level, we can move around God's Word so freely that our repertoire seems limitless. More important, we can focus our attention on the Holy Spirit's promptings and on the person we seek to serve.

> If a passion for evangelism is in your subconscious, it bleeds into everything else you do or say.

If all we know are a handful of verses, and we stumble over even those, we're like a guitarist who is limited to songs that primarily use an E minor chord (the simplest to play on a guitar), and unable to sing along at that. But if something such as a passion for evangelism is in your subconscious, it bleeds into everything else you do or say.

Having a strong foundation in God's Word is only the starting point. It's only the foundation. Unless you go further, you'll just build a silo. A silo approach to ministry goes like this:

A: "Are you a church that models forgiveness?"

B: "Yes, I taught about forgiveness on January 6."

A: "How about hope? Are you known as a church where God gives people a second chance?"

B: "Oh yes, last year we printed a little brochure called 'The God of Hope.'"

This is the worst possible way to shepherd a congregation. When your values are like a silo, each stands alone. You can build a silo around forgiveness, hope, giving, family, or anything else.

However, if something is a totem for your church, its towering stature and central importance influence everything else in the congregation.

At New Hope, we want to bleed out certain values across the latticework of everything we do. If a value is part of our culture, we want people to get it so deep inside that the value becomes almost second-nature. Otherwise it is only a silo.

Leadership development is one of the values we want to bleed across everything we do. We continually teach and model the idea that whatever ministry you do at New Hope, it is important to develop others along the way.

We place so much emphasis on developing leadership potential within our church that we created a special school for advanced learning. In addition to being pastor of New Hope O'ahu, I am president of Pacific Rim Bible College (www.prbc-hawaii.edu), which is based here at New Hope. It is designed for those God is calling to ministry beyond New Hope. Its mission is "to develop Christian leaders," people who want to participate in ministry here, live out our values, and practice them to confidence. We want leadership development to be so intentional that it becomes natural. Our dream is to form each student into a skilled athlete in the area of leadership development.

> On a luxury liner passengers expect to be served, fed, and pampered. The church will never win wars with a cruise ship mentality!

Doing Church as a Team

We want to make sure that as many people as possible are involved in ministry, and that no one serves alone. I once visited an active-duty battleship. I noticed that all eight hundred sailors had a reason for being there; each person had both a job to do and a team to do it with. Working as a team, people accomplished what they could never do as individuals working alone.

Contrast this with a luxury liner, where passengers expect to be served, fed, and pampered while a crew scrambles to keep everyone happy. The church will never win wars with a cruise ship mentality! Churches should be battleships, where everyone is on call, where everyone has a responsibility, and where everyone is trying to make a difference. To win the spiritual battles a church faces, everyone must be involved.

Doing church as a team is so important at New Hope that it's the theme of our biggest churchwide conference year after year.[1] We talk about it all the time. I even wrote a book, called *Doing Church as a Team.*[2]

We model teamwork at every level. I make no secret of the way that most of my responsibilities are planned, conducted, and debriefed in connection with a team. This book was even created through the work of a small team.

Gracious Spirit in All Our Dealings

We once had a church leader who seemed always to notice with annoyance whenever anyone was late. He'd go up to the person—whether volunteer or staff—and say, "I thought you were committed."

Ouch. His defeatist, guilt-inducing words were destroying our culture. His five words, coupled by the tone of voice he used, undercut any teaching we did about having a gracious spirit in all we do. A leader can either be a culture setter or the vilest of culture destroyers.

A church can have all the right totems, but an inconsistent example on the part of leaders can set back or even destroy it. Bad leadership can "toxify" the soil just as surely as if someone spills gasoline in a fertile garden.

Churches need to work to protect their emotional and spiritual environments. If we say "Our culture is to encourage people," it is the leaders who must model that behavior. Leaders set the culture, safeguard it, and increase it. They want to grow the right environment and protect it.

At New Hope, we are not hard-driving leaders, but gracious, caring people. This is one of our core values.

Undying Devotion to God's Word

Too many Christians have drifted into a devotional life that depends more on prepackaged, well-worded contemporary books than on the original source, the Bible itself. Only one book is promised by the Holy Spirit to be your guide: "Your word is a lamp to my feet / And a light to my path" (Psalm 119:105). "Every part of Scripture is God-breathed and useful in one way or another—showing us truth, exposing our rebellion, correcting our mistakes, training us to live God's way. Through the Word we are put together and shaped up for the tasks God has for us" (2 Timothy 3:16–17, The Message).

This emphasis is so important that we as a church journal together (see Appendix Two) and in other ways get the Word of God to actually study us.

Living Heart-First

Around New Hope, we often say, "Correct back to heart." At issue is not how much you do, but how much heart you put into what you do. You may do something simply, but if done with the right heart God will bless it. By contrast, if you do something very well but with the temperamental and conceited attitude of a prima donna, the Holy Spirit would rather not be involved.

You may do something simply, but if done with the right heart God will bless it.

Being immersed daily in God's work without being immersed daily in God's Word can cause any well-meaning leader to degenerate into a religious drone. One of our nonnegotiables as New Hope leaders is a daily devotion to God's Word, the Bible.

The more complicated our lives and ministries become, the more we must treasure the basics. Our eternal lifeline must stay tethered to Christ, lest we fall just "as the serpent deceived Eve . . . from the simplicity and purity of devotion to Christ" (2 Corinthians 11:3). Likewise, the apostles' reminder in Acts 6:2–4 stands as a consistent sentinel for all leaders: "It is not desirable for us to neglect the word of God . . . therefore . . . we will devote ourselves to prayer and to the ministry of the word." Your discontent can become your god.

It's best to grow at the rate at which your heart can grow. If your growth outpaces your heart, the result is burnout. Remember the African baggage carriers? If your heart isn't fully devoted to Christ, you won't be able to live heart-first. Finding yourself more preoccupied with technical perfection than with healthy relationships signals the need for immediate correction.

> Your discontent can become your god.

CHURCH *as a* LIVING ORGANISM

What kind of culture does your church have? What would the people of your church say are its totems? Can you identify the totems? Do your leaders integrate them into their daily lives? Are they the right ones for the vision and mission God has given to your church?

If you bring forth the right culture, it will change your church—and your world.

Culture Setters

A GREENHOUSE IS AN ENVIRONMENT IN WHICH PLANTS can grow, protected from the harsh weather outside. Living organisms that would otherwise wither and die instead become fruitful and healthy.

A greenhouse is also a good image for thinking about church. Such qualities are often much more important than brick-and-mortar ones.

Lately I've been realizing the importance of this greenhouse culture on the spirit of New Hope Christian Fellowship O'ahu. Within this culture, joy is experienced, laughter is heard, mistakes are readily dealt with, and people find forgiveness.

Culture setters are the people in a church who shape this all-important ambiance or environment. Typically they have leadership roles, and they serve as culture "sentries"—whether they mean to or not. The greater their leadership, the greater their influence. They set the culture in everything they do, from preaching and teaching to one-on-one conversation.

YOU REPRODUCE WHAT YOU ARE

The most important lesson I've learned over the years is that you teach what you know, but you reproduce what you are through your character and example. Culture setters often *speak* their values ("We want to build a culture marked by healthy relationships"), but their most durable impact is in what they *are*.

As I think of ways to increase the healthy greenhouse culture of New Hope, I know it begins with me. If I slump, so will the church. If I have a nonchalant, shoulder-shrugging attitude toward problems, I only exacerbate them. If I am unexcited to see people, I set a task-focused culture in motion that is difficult to change.

On the other hand, if other leaders and I set the culture correctly—which for us means adding more joy, hugs, expressions of appreciation, and strengthened relationships—the culture expands. More people will thrive.

I often talk with pastors and other church leaders who carry an almost burdensome level of responsibility for making things happen at their church. When I suggest that they focus instead on themselves as carriers of the spiritual culture, they usually voice a great sense of relief. "You are like a black belt in the kingdom of God," I affirm. "You hold the church's future in you. You are the shaper of tomorrow's church. The church will become what you are right now."

If you want to turn up the thermostat that sets a culture for outreach, growth, appreciation, and celebration (or any other quality), then model those qualities, and grow in them personally. Who you are is far more important than what you do.

> The church will become what you are right now.

Hosea observed a relationship of "like priest, like people" (Hosea 4:9). This means that if you want tomorrow's church to be healthy in its marriages, then you need a healthy marriage yourself. If you want the congregation to be a hub of leadership development, then you need to put priority on developing a handful of other leaders. If you want the congregation to become more caring, then you must model care one-on-one as well as on whatever "platform" you erect in front of others.

Ultimately we teach what we know, but we reproduce what we are. Being a culture setter is as simple—and as hard—as that.

No Area Is Exempt

In the Hilo, Hawaii, church where I served as pastor, I was struggling with our poor financial giving. So I started preaching about giving, tithing, and seed faith. I listened to tapes about biblical stewardship and went to seminars on how to help people learn to give.

Then I realized that I was one of the poorest givers in the church. I rationalized it by saying, "I don't make very much money." It seemed that the Lord said back to me, "If you lead the way, if giving becomes part of who you are, then it will be part of what *they* are too. The church will model after *you,* more than after what you teach, if the two are different."

Whoa! I changed my mind, asking God to renew the spirit of my heart and mind. My wife and I purposed to become very generous, with a dream of becoming one of the top giving units in the church.

I didn't announce my change, because the Bible tells us to do most of our giving without telling others ("do not let your left hand know what your right hand is doing, so that your giving will be in secret"; Matthew 6:3–4). Yet after struggling for ten years in Hilo, everything changed when I chose to become a giver. Funds came in as people trusted God with their finances. We were able to do a lot of good because of the additional moneys that our congregation gave.

> The church will model after *you,* more than after what you teach.

When I moved to O'ahu and started New Hope, I continued to be a giver, and the same thing happened. Most fast-growing churches experience a lag where the giving doesn't keep pace with the growth. Not here. I'm proud of how generous our people are, from maintenance workers to the occasional millionaire in the congregation. The bulk of our funds come from people with quite ordinary incomes, but our culture is one of financial bigheartedness; it adds up to a budget that can be used to help a lot of people.

Walking my talk is like a spiritual principle. When I started to embrace it, I realized that I reproduce what I am.

SET CULTURE THROUGH WHAT SPILLS OVER

I remember an airplane flight when we landed hard and a baby woke up with jolt. I watched her face start to pucker in fear, as she anxiously looked to see how her mother was handling the rough landing. When the baby saw that her mother was fine, her puckered face returned to normal, and she soon drifted back to sleep.

The child took her cue from her mother. If the mother had been fearful, the child would have reflected that. Instead, the mother murmured soothingly, "That's all right." If the mother had been exasperated, the baby would have mirrored it.

The same is true with us as leaders: how we react in our daily life is what we reproduce. I've seen it in every church I served. No matter what I teach or how much I emphasize it in my teaching, we reproduce what we are. If I'm happy, the staff is happy. If I'm exacting, they'll be exacting. If I'm depressed or frustrated, they follow suit.

> How we react in our daily life is what we reproduce.

Suppose you as a leader want to value something but you don't have strengths in that area. Some leaders have high regard for showing mercy, for example, but their personality is not empathic. You don't have to make personal visits in a hospital to show your compassion. If your heart says, "We need to visit people in the hospital," then you'll find a way to live it out, perhaps by developing care teams to put teeth to that value.

However, if the leader says, "I don't *want* to show mercy," then a character problem is at stake. Scripture teaches all followers of Jesus, not just those with special gifts of mercy, to "be merciful, just as your Father is merciful" (Luke 6:36).

Most of the time, however, the role of culture setter is less a challenge of the will and more a matter of what spills over when we're bumped.

At our church office, as perhaps in most offices, we have a big closet for supplies—pens, staples, paper, printer cartridges, and the like. If you as a staff or volunteer need something for your ministry, the office manager unlocks the door for you, makes a note of what you take, reorders supplies as needed, and debits each department according to what it uses.

That was our plan, but like most offices, it didn't quite work that way. Our office manager allowed people to borrow her key, and she thought they were making a list of what they took on a clipboard placed in the supply room. Soon enough the supplies began running low, but very little was written on the clipboard.

To fix the problem, she decided to redo the policy. "Each department should buy its own supplies and bring the receipt to me for reimbursement," she announced. "That way we can keep track of it." Nothing she said indicated that supplies were being misused; they were just misaccounted.

Another staff member, her supervisor, told me of the policy change, thinking I'd be pleased. "I'm sure this will be a better way to keep track of expenses," he said, smiling.

I was troubled because I sensed that something far more important was at stake. I didn't think the new policy fit who we are. "We've been very intentional about creating an environment of trusting relationships," I said. "Let's not penalize our staff and volunteers for something we're administrating incorrectly."

"Don't we need a way to monitor our finances better?" he countered.

"If we're forcing everyone to make their own separate trip to Office Depot or Staples, then we're adding lots of new costs, and ultimately not saving any money," I responded.

Why did a little policy change become something I wanted to challenge? My job as "shepherd of the church of God" is to "be on the alert" (Acts 20:28, 31) for anything that destroys the church that God wants to build, or its culture. As culture setters, church leaders must be on guard that important parts of our culture aren't inappropriately changed.

A similar culture challenge showed up another time at our weekend services. A baby in our community was dying of a rare bone marrow disease. The only hope was to find someone whose blood makeup exactly matched the baby's. People could test their compatibility with the baby through a simple detection process that involved a pin prick.

A woman at New Hope heard about it and asked for an announcement to be made at our worship services, inviting people to stop by a booth after the service to do the simple pin-prick test. "Does this child go to our church?" asked the pastor who was doing announcements that day. "We have a policy that says we can't include the announcement unless they go to our church. You can understand that otherwise we'd have too many announcements."

This woman didn't understand. She was a neighbor to the family with the baby in need. She wanted to involve her church in helping a life-threatening situation.

She didn't let it go. She wrote me a note explaining how her request had been rejected and asking for us please to be involved. "This doesn't sound like New Hope," her correspondence stated. "Our church is always interested in helping people, whether they go to church or not."

She was right. The next week we made a public appeal, and something like seven hundred people responded by doing the pin-prick test.

The woman wrote me another letter, this time a lovely note. "Thank you," she said. "I knew we wanted to be part of our community."

Unfortunately, the child died about three weeks later. None of our people had matched. Nor did anyone else through other avenues the parents tried.

What a setback it would have been if we hadn't tried our best to be involved. Our message would have been incongruent with the culture we were trying to build.

From one perspective, of course, it makes sense not to have dozens of announcements during a worship service, and to come up with a way of limiting the number of announcements. On the other hand, the leader's role as culture setter means we need to pay attention to make sure that what we actually do matches what we *say* we're trying to do.

Holy Spirit *as* Culture Setter

Leaders, called for a season to a church, exemplify the church's culture through their lifestyle. But as Chapter Six explained, the ultimate culture setter is the Holy Spirit. If you have a good Biblical culture, one that's delightful to the Holy Spirit, it won't be so much leader-driven as Spirit-driven. It's a divine partnership.

It's up to you to decide how much of the Spirit's leadership you will allow. At one time, I attended a bunch of leadership seminars, and the main word I heard everywhere was *leadership*. So I studied the leadership books that everyone else was reading. Soon enough, New Hope became a leadership-driven church.

A sad thing happened along the way. Ever so subtly, I began treating the people Jesus had died for more as customers than as sheep. I started to think of our church finances in terms of profit and loss. I developed an attitude that assessed someone as either a "profit person" or a "loss person." The church began to take on a mutated form, where people's performance was more important than who they were.

> The culture setter makes sure that what we actually do matches what we *say* we're trying to do.

Worse, as I got caught up in this whirlpool obsession of winning and doing the right thing at the expense of people along the way, I justified it as good leadership. "After all, people expect a top-quality sound system and they won't come if they can't hear," I told myself. "So we've got to do whatever it takes to get the right stuff." In too many ways, the church functioned just like a business.

The Holy Spirit could have been a hundred miles away from us, and it wouldn't have made a difference. A friend said to me, "I bet you could take the Holy Spirit away from half the U.S. churches, and no one would notice."

Uh-oh, I thought. *That's us.*

I stopped looking at people as customers, and empty seats as lost profits. I gave up my pursuit of the latest buzzwords as the best way to reach the community. I examined my motives for why I wanted us to have attention-grabbing advertising and offer better "customer service." The bottom line in the corporate world is that you entice listeners through better advertisement in order to get more profit. Most businesses do it only to get more money.

My teaching began to change, and I corrected myself, back to the cross as my greatest model, rather than corporate America.

> I corrected myself, back to the cross as my greatest model, rather than corporate America.

Today my greatest fear is not that I'll fall into marital problems or illegal drug use. The greatest potential damage I could do is if God took his hand away from my ministry. At that point, whatever church I'm leading would become nothing more than a business. Spirit leadership would yield to human leadership. Growing God's kingdom would be replaced by building a comfortable or prestigious lifestyle.

If I ever think this distinction doesn't matter, I reflect back on a kid named Jamie. Years ago, I was a soccer coach through Youth with a Mission. I picked up Jamie every Wednesday morning for three months. One winter morning, he got into my car, looked at me begrudgingly, and asked, "Coach, I know you're taking me to these Bible studies, and you know I'm not a Christian. Would you pick me up every week if I never become a Christian?"

The question stopped me in my tracks. I had to think! As I prayed about what to say, the Lord nailed me.

I looked Jamie in the eye and said, "Yes I would." Three months later, something happened in his heart and he received Christ. Today, he's grown up and married, and together with his wife he is serving God.

Long ago, Jamie was trying to find out, "Do you want my scalp?" It's the church-as-business question brought home: Was I serving him in order to get him saved, or would I love him just as much if he rejected Jesus?

In the corporate world, you do customer service to increase profits. If not, few companies would offer customer service. In church, we do a form of customer service and keep doing it because of our love for Christ. Period. My experience with Jamie was a big moment for me to change the way I look at people. The more recent experience that I mentioned applied the same concept to church when my friend asked, in effect, whether I'd notice if the Holy Spirit left our church.

> My friend asked whether I'd notice if the Holy Spirit left our church.

HUMAN PERSONALITY MORE THAN *the* SPIRIT

If I develop a church in such a way that people say it's "Wayne's world," then it's not a biblical culture; it will disappear like an annual flower snuffed out by the change of season. "The grass withers, the flower fades, but the word of our God stands forever" (Isaiah 40:8). If the Holy Spirit shapes the culture, then it will continue after the leader is gone. Likewise, if the senior leader *alone* embodies the culture, then once he or she moves on the church will experience culture shock. So it's important to build an environment of transgenerational leadership, and of multiple leadership.

I have seen those whose ministry no longer exists because it was built strongly on a personality or style of structure. At a faith-movement church on one of the other islands here in Hawaii, the whole culture was built on the idea that if you pray hard enough, God will do the miracles you name. "You've got to believe and have faith, and God will answer," the people told each other. They carried this idea to the point of dysfunction, where the Holy Spirit seemed more controlled than in control.

Then the wife of the senior pastor came down with cancer. The church's reaction was to keep casting out the demon of cancer. They did it again and again, but she got worse and died. Even at the funeral, they were trying to raise her out of the coffin. Apparently the Lord had decided to take her home, but they didn't let God be God. It so devastated their faith that the church closed its doors about six months later. The culture was built on a human leadership style, not on a biblical one.

The situation was so radical that it left an indelible mark on my life, to make sure everything I form will outlive me. I want to teach our congregation to be people of reality—not to have fair-weather faith, but to go through the storms of life without shipwrecking their faith. I saw that disaster and said, "I've got to make sure the Holy Spirit is truly in charge."

GETTING YOUR EDGE BACK

In the movie *Rocky III,* a boxer named Rocky Balboa has lost his edge and needs to get it back. The plot begins with Rocky as an established world-title-holding champion who fights only against weaker, underqualified opponents. Most of the time he enjoys an easy, complacent life of fame. Then an arrogant, well-trained challenger savagely beats him, accidentally landing a fatal punch on Rocky's trainer. Having lost both his title and his mentor, Rocky loses heart and wants to quit.

Church leaders need the eye of the tiger as well.

Another fighter, Apollo Creed, talks to Rocky about recovering "the eye of the tiger"—his decisive fighting spirit, the hunger and need to give his all. Eventually Rocky finds the eye of the tiger and returns to his training with renewed vigor. Rocky then goes for a rematch, which proves to be the challenge of his lifetime, and he wins.

Church leaders need the eye of the tiger as well. We've got to be so in love with the church that we are pouring our hearts into it.

Even though I write books and like to travel, church is my life. It isn't a laboratory for experimentation, or an employer that gives me a paycheck, so much as a people and culture that I love.

When I'm on autopilot, with my mind or heart elsewhere, I can't be the culture setter at New Hope. By losing the eye of the tiger, as the movie soundtrack says, "You trade your passion for glory" and you quit "rising up to the challenge." You play church by going through the motions and being content with mediocrity.

As I walk with God, he motivates me to long for biblical culture and not settle into a comfortable life as Rocky did. Instead, God stirs me to identify our totems (basic principles), live them, and communicate them. With the Spirit's enabling, I want to end the contests of this life having given it my all, able to say with the Apostle Paul, "I have fought the good fight, I have finished the course, I have kept the faith; in the future there is laid up for me the crown of righteousness, which the Lord, the righteous Judge, will award to me on that day; and not only to me, but also to all who have loved His appearing" (2 Timothy 4:7–8).

Suppose you're 5'1", had asthma as a child, and have zero hope of ever being mistaken for Rocky (or Xena the Warrior Princess). Do these verses apply to you, spiritually speaking?

Good news: you don't have to be a towering personality like Focus on the Family's James Dobson to be a culture setter. If you can get the right culture going, stuff grows on its own. It's like allowing an orchard to grow, rather than one person mandating that it must grow.

I remember a pastor who gave testimony at a conference our church sponsored. He shared some wonderful miracles of a home whose family life was transformed by the love of his church. It was irrelevant (and I'll never know anyway) whether his was a church of seventy, or seven hundred, or seven thousand in attendance. The point has nothing to do with size, but with how lives are being transformed. My response was to thank God. I thought, "This world needs every single church we've got! Each has a purpose, niche, and role to play.

If each of us has the right culture, then all of us together as a team can do 'capital C' Church."

We need to have every church be doing well. God doesn't require you to be Eddie Long, Beth Moore, or any other spiritual superstar. As long as you're someone intentional about setting a biblical culture, then together we're advancing the kingdom of God.

Plug-and-Play Subculture
vs. Authentic Culture

I ONCE ASKED NEW HOPE CHRISTIAN FELLOWSHIP O'ahu to hire a talented worship leader. His personality on the platform during services came across impressively, but off stage he was abrasive. As talented musicians came in the front door of the church, they would encounter him and quickly head out the back door.

It wasn't just because they saw that he was terribly disorganized and had a family that was a mess. Instead, he *meant* to push people away. We had a great music program. But whenever people were attracted by it and wanted to get involved, he would find some way to disqualify them or tell them he had no room.

The difficulty was not the aspiring musicians or our many-layered music program, but him. He didn't want anyone around who might be as good as he was. He was insecure and didn't want them to show him up.

He was destroying New Hope's rich culture of recruiting new people as emerging leaders. He was building his own kingdom, which is just the opposite of how we value teamwork and developing others at New Hope.

At the same time, there was an even deeper problem present. It was not this new worship leader, but me. I had learned about a church that brought on a superstar worship leader, and they were growing faster than we were. "If we do that too, we'll grow like they did," I told myself. So I found myself playing a spiritual version of keeping up with the Joneses. I hired the talented but unpleasant worship leader in order to draw more people and grow the church. I felt that New Hope wasn't growing quickly enough, and so I made a somewhat impulsive response.

Our new worship leader was not the only person with insecurities. I was too. I was fearful that my preaching wouldn't be able to carry enough weight as God kept growing the church. Could my preaching rise to new levels? I wasn't confident it could. In my preaching insecurities, I told myself, "If I can ramp up New Hope's worship with our own Darlene Zschech, Chris Tomlin, or Michael W. Smith, then I won't have to work so hard in my preaching."

Two years later, I had to ask the worship leader to step down. We had lost too many people who could have been a wonderful addition to our church. Ultimately, they held back because I was too impetuous and too insecure in my own leadership.

Subculture Seems Easier

One way we grow the right culture at New Hope is to guard against an unhealthy subculture. I use the word *subculture* to describe what developed during those two years. I dropped another church's approach onto New Hope's culture, treating it like a plug-and-play component on a stereo. When we plugged it into our system, I assumed that it would play for us the same way it had for the other church. I didn't think through how it might challenge or change New Hope's totems, creating an alternate culture.

When church leaders feel desperate, as I did ("we need help"), and especially if the timing is urgent ("we need a new program within the next few weeks"), we often seek a quick fix through a plug-and-play approach. My concern today is that, over the next decade, many churches will continue making the same mistake I did at New Hope: allowing such a mentality and approach to birth a subculture.

It's easy to resort to finding something we can copy. But if a church's most comfortable decision is to search out and copy yet another program, it's in danger of forming a huge subculture. Some church subcultures depend on a never-ending series of patches, coming to view them as the normal way of doing church.

Indeed, turnkey programs are available everywhere. They flourish in churches, just as get-rich-quick schemes proliferate on commercial television. They offer a church a lot in a short time. We've all heard the sensational promises that you can build a world-class vocabulary in thirty days and immediately obtain a new, executive-level, high-paying job. It's far more likely that we'll learn only a few words and make only a small but noticeable step of progress, yet we fall for the instant-gratification lure anyway. In a world of instantaneous messaging on the computer and instant coffee making in the kitchen, we want immediate results in our churches.

Many programs used in this way are outstanding in themselves. They are rooted in Scripture. God has blessed them abundantly in the churches that birthed them. They have the potential, if properly tailored, to be a great instrument of God in your church and mine.

What's the downside of a program-driven clone? The biggest danger is the attitude that we can copy another ministry in a one-size-fits-all approach without creating a knotty subculture.

> When church leaders feel desperate, and especially if the timing is urgent, we often seek a quick fix through a plug-and-play approach.

EASIER *to* DUPLICATE THAN *to* INCARNATE

What's so unhealthy about a subculture formed from cloning another church's approach? In duplicating, you don't need to think creatively.

> The biggest danger
> is the attitude
> that we can copy
> another ministry
> in a one-size-fits-all
> approach without
> creating a knotty
> subculture.

Programs don't require much innovation. You aren't looking to God for new insights, horizons, vistas. You're simply copying another program or leader. You become someone without much imagination or vision.

In times of desperation, it's easier to duplicate than to incarnate. It's easier to do a plug-and-play ministry than to do the hard work of personalizing Jesus to our particular situation.

Jesus promised that "he who believes in me, the works that I do, he will do also; and greater works than these he will do . . ." (John 14:12). Those greater works, as he explained, happen as we allow the Holy Spirit to empower, teach, and guide us.

The Holy Spirit works in the arena of faith. The Spirit wants you to be willing to step over the edge and float on thin air. The great saints of old learned to walk by way of promises, not through someone else's program. They learned that "faith is the assurance of things hoped for, the conviction of things not seen" (Hebrews 11:1–2). As Joshua, they led others to new places, reminding them to depend on God because "you have not passed this way before" (Joshua 3:4). They pressed ahead, believing "eye has not seen and ear has not heard . . . all that God has prepared" (1 Corinthians 2:9). They knew that to live by God's promises they had to hear the Spirit and be led step-by-step.

As church leaders merely duplicate someone else's vision, they diminish their innovative, creative, and entrepreneurial side. Their gears become frozen; so long as they focus on copying someone else's ministry, they don't learn to get the stuck gears going.

If you don't live by God's promises, you'll never advance and grow. You'll clone, continue, duplicate, and maintain. Building by program is faster, but it doesn't last. Programs build a presence but not a future. Building with programs means building a subculture for today, but building your unique culture releases your future.

In moving with the innovation of the Spirit to develop new vistas, you say, "Lord, we've not gone that way before, but we need to hear the Spirit speak to us." You look at the people in your church and understand why God put them there. You recognize that there are thousands of people in your community yet to be reached. You rejoice in the resources available to you, agreeing that God "is able to do far more abundantly beyond all that we ask or think [the New International Version translates this word *imagine*] according to the power that works within us . . ." (Ephesians 3:20–21).

Something isn't working when we see churches continuing what they're doing and never noticing that the Holy Spirit didn't show up.

We need an innovative edge to spiritual leadership in the twenty-first century. Business as usual isn't changing the world. Something isn't working when we see churches closing and too many others continuing just what they're doing and never noticing that the Holy Spirit didn't show up. Living by promises rather than others' programs, you sense the Spirit saying to you, "This is what you're doing to destroy the culture." You also see how the Spirit wants to ignite your church. You discover afresh that no one is more creative than the Creator of the universe—and that if you can tap into him, you'll be surprised at the things he shows you.

SUBCULTURE TAKES OVER LIKE *a* WEED

Sometimes a subculture emerges not because of something we do but because of neglect. Like a vegetable garden with weeds popping up, a church left untended can allow the wrong things to grow. It's a problem of omission more than of commission.

I remember a season of neglect that began when I was invited to another city to speak to some church leaders. I couldn't have asked for a more receptive audience. But from that blessing of God, I started having wrong thoughts. The handshakes there seemed to be warmer than the ones I was getting back home. The sense of appreciation seemed greater than what I was receiving from New Hope. "These audiences really like me," I told myself. "Maybe I should become an itinerant preacher like John Maxwell or Anne Graham Lotz." Although I had spoken to outside groups since my earliest days at New Hope, this was the first time I began looking for admiration outside New Hope. It was also the moment in which I began losing my reason for being a pastor at New Hope.

Almost without realizing it, I put New Hope on autopilot so that I could tend to my aspirations. I abdicated certain responsibilities by taking the easy way: I let this program come in and take over, and I let that guest speaker or unguided staff set too much of the church's direction.

Instead of cultivating the daisies and carrots, I stood by and allowed the dandelions and stinkweed to grow. A subculture started to develop. Not surprisingly, I became discouraged with the church, sensing that things weren't going well—but not realizing that I was the gatekeeper who was allowing the wrong things to grow.

God brought me back to my senses in a most unusual way. I was invited to speak at a church conference that had a lot to teach our church, so I brought a large group of people from New Hope with me. We spent $35,000 to send our team (which was well worth it). I put a great deal of work into my message preparation, spoke many times during our time there, gave them my all, and received no letter of thanks or honorarium. They didn't even pay for my airfare! Instead of feeling appreciated, I felt used. I felt they wanted me only for what my church and I could give to them.

Shortly after that, I traveled to speak at another church, bringing a number of my books with me for the church to sell, as they had requested. They sold all the books—and then kept the money. Coming home and realizing that I had been bilked, I asked myself, "What am I doing?" God used those experiences to nail my heart.

Like the prodigal son who concluded "My father's house is better than this pigsty" (see Luke 10:11–32), I realized that my heavenly Father's call to New Hope is far better than my aspirations to be on my own. "I don't want to be just another speaker," I thought. "I want to shepherd people and help them be fruitful." I realized that I love New Hope more than any other people.

First, realize that a shift is needed. Next, identify the culture you want to have.

Reengaging at New Hope, I took a new look around. Because I had been mentally absent for eight months, a wrong subculture was taking over; strong staff with strong opinions were nestled into niches of the ministry. I had to clean house, fire three people, and change some things around. It was pretty bloody.

The Lord said, in essence, "Choose where you want to be." He used a rich contrast of experiences to teach me where my home base was and to allow me to get my edge back. I'm so thankful I responded to God in time, because some pastors don't.

SUBCULTURE ALSO
COMES *by* STAYING STILL

Another kind of subculture, in terms of leading or building teams, is tradition—the way we've done it before. By the time a church has been around just ten or twenty years, it has a lot more traditions than many of its leaders imagine. Once a church has existed for fifty to one hundred or more years, tradition usually occupies a conspicuous front seat around any leadership development table.

Pastors of long-standing churches, where tradition is supreme, often ask how to transform their culture from the inside out.

Pastors of long-standing churches, where tradition is supreme, often ask how to transform their culture from the inside out. My reply is to affirm them: "The first step is the one you just took—realizing that a shift is needed. You've identified an incorrect or unhealthy subculture."

Next is to identify the culture they *want* to have. This occurs when they compare where they are now with their totems as a church. They must put their finger on where they want to be in three to eight years, putting specific names to each totem that needs to be there.

I can't overemphasize the importance of knowing exactly where God is calling your church to go. Imagine being given a free ticket to anywhere in the world. If you don't know where you want to go, the airline industry can't help you. The tools are there—reservation agents, suitcases, airports—but they do you little good until you decide where to go.

It requires "knee time" and the wise counsel of others, but once you do know then certain wheels start turning. Things start moving. Things fit into place once you understand the true culture the Lord wants for your church.

I don't know if it's the Holy Spirit or simply how God created the world (or both), but as soon as you identify your destination you start finding leaders who fit better, your church takes on a more positive self-image, and you have fresh clarity of direction. An intuitive transition takes place, something of an atmospheric change, a disposition, almost the way the righteousness of God took on new clarity for John, who was hesitant to baptize Jesus until he realized it was the fitting thing to do, as Jesus explained: "It must be done, because we must do everything that is right" (Matthew 3:15, NLT).

The third step is to figure out how to negotiate the turns to get there. This requires the wisdom of the Lord and the timing of several years. God wants our churches to be the kind that make an impact in the world. If we agree with God and make that our decision, something happens. All we have to do is to cooperate along the way.

THE HYBRID DETOUR

Another way of developing subculture is to hybridize your culture, borrowing from other churches but doing so such that your church loses its identity in the process. As the Christian entrepreneurial leader

Fred Smith Sr. once said to me: "Hell is one day God showing me all I could have been and never was."

It happened like this. A friend of mine who pastors another church came to Hawaii and invited me to come onto the staff of his church, perhaps even becoming his successor as senior pastor. He came to me at a time when I was pretty discouraged. Our worship attendance was flatlined from maxing out our current location, and at the time I couldn't think of any other options. We rent multiple properties for our worship services, and I had just been reviewing the overwhelming costs of a possible land purchase. I was uncertain whether New Hope could accommodate more growth, and being a pioneer by nature I was unexcited about simply maintaining the church at its present level year after year, borrowing ideas from other churches merely to keep the church running.

I was borrowing ideas from other churches merely to keep the church running.

By contrast, my friend's church was larger and more well-known, and it had all kinds of good things happening. So I was drawn into the dream of what God was doing in my friend's area.

My friend knew just how to pitch his appeal. "Wayne," he said, "if you don't think Hawaii is the right place for all the potential still inside of you, then don't squander God's gifts. Hand the baton to someone who will maintain the church, and come help us."

He had pegged me. I was starting to slacken, live on our laurels, and maintain. My next step would have been to hybridize the church, adding other churches' programs because I didn't know what else to do.

After he left, I got on my knees and said, "God, he's right, but I like the kind of people here better. I don't feel called to his part of the country, and I definitely don't like the weather there!" The Lord confirmed by showing us a creative answer to our space issues. We started doing video venues, hiving off large groups to new locations across our island. This opened up space for our main, rented high school. By expanding to as many as fifteen locations over the next ten years, we

can keep reaching new people for Christ. We can also develop plat-
forms for more leaders, as I explain elsewhere.

My friend's concluding words, as we ended our deliberation, were
a startling reminder of Fred Smith's message: "When you die, the Lord
will show you all you could have been but never were." It's scary to
think that your church or mine might never know who we were supposed to have been, all because we quit growing, began to coast, and
started to become something we're not.

Early Detection *of* Subculture Formation

The way to detect the formation of a subculture—which is critical—
is by staying personally close to God. It sounds so simple. If we're staying faithful in devotions, the Word of God starts to point out where
we are cutting corners.

If we're duplicating rather than incarnating, and cloning rather
than following God's assignment for our particular church, we start
to develop a subculture. God uses his Word to challenge our motives.
"The word of God is living and active and sharper than any two-edged
sword, and piercing as far as the division of soul and spirit, of both
joints and marrow, and able to judge the thoughts and intentions of
the heart" (Hebrews 4:12). So when I'm sitting before the Lord, he
actually checks the thoughts and intentions in my heart, lays bare my
soul, and studies me.

Any Christian leader, empowered by God's Spirit and walking
daily by faith, will have an artesian well of ideas. We'll be like quar-
terbacks able to call "audibles" on the line of scrimmage: a new or substitute play made as a spontaneous adjustment to how the opposition
has formed. This well of incarnation enables a church to become vibrant, current, future-building, and culture-releasing. Lots of churches
are caught instead in program redundancy. A pity, because it's actually easier in the long run (not to mention smarter too!) to tap into
the artesian source of the Word of God.

10

Creating and Re-Creating Culture

MAINLANDERS VISITING NEW HOPE O'AHU OFTEN ask me, "Is Hawaii a culture where people love each other all the time?" Many have a stereotype of Hawaii's residents as always happy, relaxed, singing songs, handing out leis, and offering hugs. It's easy to imagine these values as naturally occurring in our church ("You hug each other at New Hope, and everyone is unusually kind to each other, but isn't that inborn, part of the Hawaiian culture?").

Unfortunately, that's not always how we are, even though hospitality is certainly part of our Polynesian heritage. We also have neighborhoods riddled with gangs and graffiti. Hawaii has perhaps the highest domestic abuse rate in the country. Use of crystal methamphetamine, or "ice," is at an epidemic level. We're dealing with major prostitution, especially among minors, with our rate of juvenile female arrests reaching record proportions. We have old problems such as racial prejudice, and new problems such as violence among surfers, with people beating each other up merely to get a wave!

Hawaiians are loving and kind toward tourists because we depend on your money, but we're certainly not always a culture where everybody is loving and kind. If you like what you experience at New Hope and you dismiss it as "Well, this is Hawaii," then you don't know all sides of Hawaii. You may imagine our climate as heavenly, but our culture does have some drawbacks that heaven doesn't.

The lifeblood of New Hope is a culture we've been quite intentional about forming. If we can build a desirable culture here, then you can do likewise with creating a unique culture in your community. It's like Nashville's Opryland Hotel, which I described at the beginning of Chapter Seven. If engineers and architects can physically construct a hotel with a life-supporting culture, then we can spiritually foster a similar organic culture in our churches, whether in Honolulu or anywhere else.

Social scientists have told us, "You're just a product of your environment." That's partly true. But if you're a leader, your church's environment should be a product of the work of God through you. You don't need to be a chameleon, changing to look like whatever culture surrounds you. You also don't need to feel victimized and decide you have no control over what happens at your church.

> If you're a leader, your church's environment should be a product of the work of God through you.

You develop the culture as an outgrowth of three factors: your teaching, your attitude, and how you think. Whatever you believe God wants the church to be, you become it first, being genuine to your core.

As the culture setter, what is the process you go through to set the culture? Let me describe what we did at New Hope to help our people be fruitful, and how we now advance it.

Developing *a* Culture *of* Love

At New Hope, we are developing a culture of love, where people genuinely care for one another.

We like to imagine that everyone has a nametag that reads, "Hello, my name is _____. Please help me feel valuable today." If you treat people as God does, their souls will be touched.

Many of our telephone receptionists are volunteers. I learned of one volunteer who has a day job six days a week but then volunteers at our New Hope switchboard on her one day off. "Why do you come here and do this?" I asked her.

"Being here is like a breath of fresh air," she replied.

"Don't you want to take a day off?"

"This *is* a day off," she responded. "It fills my soul."

She feels valued. That's the kind of love we want to show.

This love is not something we muster on our own. It comes from learning to recognize evidence of God's presence. It's easy to look for evidence of God's absence, but we focus on the opposite because we know that people tend to see whatever they look for. If I decide to buy a certain type of car, I suddenly see it everywhere I look. My reticular activating system (RAS) filters out unwanted things— the dozens of car models that I'm not looking for. At New Hope we try to activate our spiritual RAS, knowing that if we're not looking for Jesus we won't see him.

> If you treat people as God does, their souls will be touched.

We want to be like Zacchaeus, who "wanted desperately to see Jesus" (Luke 19:3, The Message). As he did with Zacchaeus, Jesus stops and turns to those who seek him.

We want to be like the woman with a twelve-year ongoing medical problem who was determined to break through the crowd and touch Jesus' garment. When she did and Jesus responded, the disciples questioned how Jesus could notice that someone had touched him, since a large crowd was surrounding him. He replied, in essence, "There's a big difference between people bumping into me and someone touching me" (see Luke 8:43–48).

Too often in our churches we're bumping into Jesus, but no one is intentionally touching him.

Developing *a* Culture *of* Learning *and* Correction

The Bible says, "Tell good people what you know—they'll profit from it" (Proverbs 9:9, The Message) and "The wisdom of the wise keeps life on track; the foolishness of fools lands them in the ditch" (Proverbs 14:8, The Message).

If you don't debrief what you do through a life-on-life discussion, how will you improve? We assess everything we do through feedback, as Jesus modeled in Luke 10:1–24. We try to do it in a way that encourages and builds each other up. The last thing we want to do is to raise a penal code ("You'll lose this job if you mess up" or "You're less valuable to us if you blow it"). Anytime we focus on performance alone, we shrink hearts. Instead, we model questions such as "How could we improve for next time?" and attitudes that sincerely say "We're willing to change whatever is needed."

Too often in our church we're bumping into Jesus, but no one is intentionally touching him.

Whenever our people become defensive, resentful, or upset that we're "always" changing stuff, we know we've missed something. It's an indicator that we need to emphasize a culture of learning. It's a sign that I need to sit longer with them and let them know how valuable they are.

Suppose a volunteer starts serving as our church's new wedding coordinator. She tries to dispel everyone's nervousness through constant use of humor, but I sense that it disrespects the formality of the occasion.

I might say: "The wedding really went well. Thank you for caring for them and putting so much heart and preparation into the wedding. May I suggest something small that would make it even better next time?"

If she is hesitant or resistant, then I hold my suggestion and affirm her more. If she's teachable, then I can explain the sense of formality that's sacred to most weddings. "You want to allow that heightened sense of respect, so maybe watch how much humor you use," I might conclude.

If it works, she will see me not as a corrector but as a mentor, pastor, and friend. Otherwise I leave people bloodied, and after a while they don't want to be corrected.

Remember that it's painful to be corrected. Whenever I correct someone ("Bob, you've got to stop being late") I'm pulling something away from Bob, such as a flaw or an immaturity. I'm probably also ripping out a few roots that come with it. After a while Bob shies away because he's tired of bleeding. He hides the next time he sees me coming.

Unless we build the culture otherwise, most people will assume that when they're corrected they're being devalued. Instead, I want to have enough relationship and trust with Bob that he sees my correction as someone investing in him. I want him to develop the receptivity reflected in a proverb: "About face! I can revise your life. Look, I'm ready to pour out my spirit on you . . ." (Proverbs 1:23, The Message).

When the congregation has that kind of heart, the Holy Spirit can have carte blanche in the church. Otherwise the Spirit may sit on the sideline and say, "When you're ready for me, let me know."

My goal in correcting is to add greater value than what I take away. It's just the opposite of the museum thief who takes the gem off its pedestal while preventing the alarm from going off by substituting a bag of sand that's calculated to the same weight. By contrast, I want to displace the sand in someone's life and replace it with a diamond!

I might say, "You're doing an A-plus job, but may I share an idea that would raise it even higher?" If I've cultivated the right culture, the person will genuinely welcome the conversation.

DEVELOPING *a* CULTURE
of CREATING SPACE

It's important to make room for people to try ministry without being punished for falling short, and to stretch their wings without fear of being permanently grounded if they crash.

The delicacy in creating room, pushing back parameters, is that some people will misunderstand and think we're diluting our standards. Actually, we're just allowing a controlled explosion!

For example, suppose your youth group prepares a hip-hop presentation in order to reach other kids. You might create space for them with this introduction: "I'm so glad we have a church that loves youths. More than any group I know, this church allows them to develop, and then to consecrate their skills for Jesus, letting God redeem their talents. So today instead of dancing in the streets, they're dancing before the throne of God. Won't you welcome our newest youth dance group?"

By doing so, you're not diluting your church's boundaries but creating space. The elders are less likely to come and fuss because you've asked them to be open to this experiment. You've also shown how the innovation ties into the church's unique culture (sometimes called its spiritual DNA).

I once asked the drum line at the University of Hawaii if they'd like to play for God. "How would we do that?" one of the drummers replied. "I'd like you to open our Easter services with your drums," I explained, referring to the trashcans-for-drums approach in the musical *Stomp*. About fifteen of them said yes. They brought in many sorts of trashcans to use as drums, practiced with us, and then played on Easter with all their heart. We even developed a multicolored visual backdrop to pulsate in rhythm to their drum "prelude." I tied my message on the God of new beginnings into how we sometimes feel as if we're nothing but trash.

After the service, I asked the drummers how they liked it. One replied, "No church has ever allowed us to do this." I smiled and replied, "Well you found one that does." He was still learning how churches work so he asked, "Can we come again, or do we have to be members first?" I welcomed them to return. Since then a couple of them have received the Lord into their lives.

I later received this critical letter: "Dear Pastor Wayne: I'm writing because I attended your Easter service on Sunday morning. I found the service pathetic and uncomfortable. People banging trash cans on stage and the multicolored screen on stage made me feel like I was on acid—give me a break! Services like this are the reason I no longer attend. If I wanted to see a Superbowl halftime, I'd watch that."

I'm sorry we lost him, but we're not for everyone. What we did was consistent with our values, especially our first priority of connecting everything we do to a soul. People came to Christ. Many others said it fed their souls. We honored God through creativity.

Our object is never to try something new as an end in itself, but to bear fruit through the space we open. Jesus says in John 15:8 that we honor God when we "bear much fruit and so prove to be my disciples."

Developing *a* Culture *of* Apprenticeship

Anyone hanging around New Hope will hear the terms *mentoring* and *coaching* and phrases such as "doing church as a team" and "developing your fractal" (a small group of about four). There is constant reference to the priority Jesus put on disciple making, and frequent mention of verses such as 2 Timothy 2:2: "You have heard me teach many things that have been confirmed by many reliable witnesses. Teach these great truths to trustworthy people who are able to pass them on to others" (NLT).

The underlying attitude is that each of us lives to make others successful. We want to set up others for success. No one should feel left alone in ministry. We each want to develop skills for helping someone get to the next step in ministry. If we know someone can't handle a full sermon or a week-to-week responsibility, then we set up a rotation or tag team. If we know someone has a great heart but isn't fully up to speed musically, we put them in a group or ensemble.

> The underlying attitude is that each of us lives to make others successful.

Likewise we help leaders learn how to help people grow in their faith. If a married couple has a great testimony of something God did, then maybe we'll work with them to create a video, or interview them. Maybe we'll prime you by saying, "Tell me two stories of how your life changed because of . . ." At each step, we model ways to be a minister maker.

Sometimes people say, "So-and-so is in my ministry and has a bad disposition." The problem is one of perception. If we want veteran, mature Christians only, we will have fewer problems. Usually the problem itself is not nearly as important as our attitude and perception of it. When a poor attitude surfaces, we view it as an invitation for ministry, an opportunity to correct back to heart. For us at New Hope, attitude is everything. We hire for attitude and we fire for attitude, and with volunteers we continually work on attitude.

When life gets complex and fast, relationships wither. We want to be minister makers, and that requires people to be invested in each other.

Because of the assignment of this church to plant new churches, we need an unending flow of new, emerging leaders. We give it priority, time, money, and staffing. We also have many levels of intern programs.

PRACTICAL STEPS *to* MAKING CULTURAL TOTEMS KNOWN

If these are our cultural totems, then how do we make them known? At New Hope we take five steps:

1. Live them as qualities we are, more than as a program we do.
2. Bleed them into sermons and other public messages.
3. Link them to our mission statement as we talk about them.
4. Post them in conspicuous places (for us, it's on the walls of our office).
5. Hold everyone accountable to them.

When we practice all five, our culture comes alive; everyone has the same spirit. Our environment becomes not a program but a true culture.

I give immediate attention to the first sign that any of our totems are being destroyed by a leader who is living inconsistently. One afternoon I came into my office to find my executive assistant in tears. "What happened?" I asked, but she was reluctant to tell me. Finally, after much coaxing, she told me that one of our members had come into the church office the day before and been very harsh with her, demanding to see me.

"You know where he is. I need you to put me in touch with him today," he insisted.

She asked about his circumstances; it was not an emergency. She decided (rightly so) that this did not warrant tracking me down or calling me into the office.

After hearing her story, I immediately phoned this guy. "Eddie [not his real name], I heard you were here at my office," I said.

"That's right, and you weren't."

"I'm sorry. I was off-island," I commented. "I'm here today if you'd like to see me."

"I already told your secretary I wanted to see you," he said.

"Yes, and you made her cry, didn't you?"

"I didn't mean to upset her that much."

"Eddie, you were harsh with her."

"I wanted to see you, and she was holding out on me."

"Listen, Eddie," I continued, "God has a mantle on you, but if you become demanding like that, you will never see that mantle realized. People will not feel comfortable with your leadership if you demand rather than serve, and if you demean rather than lift up."

He was silent.

"Eddie, I love you too much to let you disqualify yourself. I'd love to see you grow in your leadership responsibilities, but that won't happen unless you reconcile what you just did. I want you to ask forgiveness from my assistant, and to do it soon."

He hesitated. "Well, ummm."

He met with her on Sunday, and cried in genuine contrition. Today Eddie is an elder and board member. He also teaches in our Bible College.

Healthy relationships are critical to any culture that is biblical and God-honoring. We keep our values in plain view. We offer pictures of people and their relationships. We celebrate the culture that God is forming in our midst.

How *to* Transition *a* Culture

At New Hope, everything we do is culture-building. We're always asking the question of how to transition the culture from where it is to where it needs to be. Would this be the same case if I were at another church, one with many years of history and tradition?

These are the steps I advise others to follow when they are changing churches:

1. Like a big, red "You are here" arrow at each different entrance of a mall, find out where the you-are-here pointer is for your church, on the basis of its DNA background. Warning: the locator is probably in a different place from where it was in the church you last came from. It may take a year or two to find the you-are-here pointer. If you don't find it, and you start as if you're coming from another direction, you'll lose a lot of people because they won't be able to follow.

Healthy relationships are critical to any culture that is biblical and God-honoring.

2. Define and establish a definite purpose of ministry. What does God want this church to do and be? From that, what would you say is your overarching, God-given assignment at this church for the next five to ten years? Write it down. At New Hope, ours is to build a model church, develop emerging leaders, and build a presence such that the community says they're glad we're here. This means we'll need to be a church that thinks out of the box, imaginatively and creatively, but with all heart and rooted in God's Word. Using the mall direction-board illustration, this means you are trying to find Sears, Radio Shack, or Nordstrom.

3. Write down the rewards that will emerge if you get to your destination. Hebrews 11:6 says God "is a rewarder of those who seek Him." We want to raise the bar and proclaim that Jesus is alive and has something relevant to say to businesspersons, homemakers, children and youths, athletes, and those well known in our community. The rewards are that people will be saved, churches will grow, and the awareness of Christ will be raised across our state and beyond. To us, if it's worth one soul, it's worth it all. Hebrews also says: "Do not throw away your confidence, which has a great reward" (Hebrews 10:35).

4. Associate as closely as possible with those who are in sympathy with your assignment, so they can encourage and help you. Line up as many allies as you can. Develop a small group (at New Hope we call it a fractal group, as I mentioned earlier) of those who become genuine friends. When you say "I need help," their first response is "You bet; what do you need?" An alliance of people like that also serves as a sideview mirror, enabling you to see your blind spots.

5. Every day, make a move toward your destination. Have a meeting, recruit a leader, do a teaching, write an article, make a phone call; somehow, act on it. As Jesus said to the Roman centurion, "Go your way; and as you have believed, so let it be done for you" (Matthew 8:13, NKJV). Prune out passive faith—anything you're not acting on.

6. Privately and personally, look for a pacesetter who is ahead of you, and then ask God for grace to surpass even that person. Follow a model that will push you and help you do your best. As part of a team from New Hope, I've participated in a forty-two-mile, six-man canoe race off the island of Molokai. It's brutal, lasting five or six hours. We know the team that has beat us, and we pace ourselves by them, desiring to surpass even them. I apply this same motivation at church. Elisha sought from Elijah, "Please, let a double portion of your spirit be upon me" (2 Kings 2:9). According to Hebrews 12:1, "Since we are surrounded by such a great cloud of

> Every day, make a move toward your destination. Prune out passive faith—anything you're not acting on.

witnesses, let us throw off everything that hinders and the sin that so easily entangles, and let us run with perseverance the race marked out for us."

OPPORTUNITIES *to* RE-CREATE *the* CULTURE

I once went with a friend to dive for *tako* (Japanese for octopus). It's a relatively simple procedure. You put on a snorkeling mask and hold a spear in your hand as you float along the surface of the water. As soon as you see an octopus, you dive quickly because they are fast and hide swiftly. My friend explained how to identify the holes they hide in, and how they wrap around your spear if you set it along the entrance to their hiding place.

We got out in the water, each with spear in hand. Within seconds, my friend dove down, brought one up, put it into our bag, and smiled, thinking about the good dinner we were going to have. Meanwhile I was still looking for my first octopus.

He got in position again and we dove down; almost immediately he came up with another octopus. Then another. And another.

"I didn't see that!" I called out in frustration.

Without commenting, he went down again and brought up another, and another, and another. I was counting, and noticed the conspicuous difference between us. He had eight while I had found none.

Finally I blurted out, "How in the world can you see them?"

"Wayne," he replied, "they're all over there!"

"No," I said, "it's a desert down there, just sand and coral."

"No way; it's abundant, they're all over. It's like a goldmine," he said almost laughing, as he dove to get one more.

In the same way, if you train your eyes and heart to see opportunities to create and re-create the culture at your church, you will see a goldmine. Where others may see a desert, your eye will look around and conclude, like my friend with the ocean full of octopus, that opportunities are all over the place.

Growing the Culture at Fellowship Bible Church

MORE THAN FIFTEEN YEARS AGO, FELLOWSHIP Bible Church partnered with several other churches to launch a seminary for church planting in a country whose population is largely unreached by evangelical Christians. One of the challenges we faced is that the number of people worldwide who speak their language is less than 0.1 percent of the world's population. As a result, professors and students are extremely limited in the number of available Christian books they can access in their own language, from Bible commentaries and scholarly journals to practical tools and various reports about what is happening in today's church around the globe.

Our solution was to require professors and students to learn English, which has more printed resources and Internet pages than any other language. In this way, they could better explore not only the Bible but also how God is working in and around the world today. Indeed, this exposure opened new windows to them for seeing new possibilities, thinking in new ways, cultivating new ideas, and hearing about "what else" the Holy Spirit is doing in his church.

A few years down the road, however, the seminary opted to relax the two-language requirement. Soon both professors and students spoke only the national language. As a result, they restricted themselves and their futures. Now the only paradigm they had regular access to for doing church was their own, and much of it was old, outdated, and ineffective. Sadly, the less they saw of other approaches, the better their own rather disheartening models looked.

From time to time, our church sends our members to visit the seminary. Much of what they see encourages them, but they also report, "Our friends aren't aware of certain laity-equipping models of ministry. Why aren't they exposed to more approaches?"

The answer is simple: they have only one language with which to see the world.

Unfortunately, many North American churches have the same problem. They too have only one language for doing church. It's the language of outside-in. It's the external approach that keeps reaching for the most recent innovation or the latest new program as a way to solve their problems or advance their ministries.

As good as many of these tools are, often they actually restrict these churches and their future. What these churches really need is to learn to speak another language: the language of inside-out, the language of culture. Only then will their eyes be open to what the Holy Spirit wants for them. Only then will they stop holding themselves back with "good things" borrowed from somewhere else, while overlooking the "best things" that are often right in front of them.

* * * * *

Part Four tells the story of Robert's experiences with culture shift at Fellowship Bible Church. Although Arkansas is quite different from Hawaii, and Robert's church differs from Wayne's, we think you'll see some parallels in their experiences.

Identifying Fellowship Bible's Totems

I WAS ONCE ASKED FOR THE LONG-RANGE VISION OF our church. "It's our values," I spontaneously answered. That's true. Everything we do at Fellowship Bible Church is shaped and developed in some way with our values clearly in mind.

So what *core* values drive and shape the people of Fellowship? What is it that immediately calls our congregation to attention, ignites our passion, and brings forth a salute? What are our "to die for's"?

Almost anyone at Fellowship, if asked those questions, could readily identify our strongest energy-driving forces. They're considered central and essential to who we are.

Most important, we believe these values are the ones God brought to us rather than something we thought up on our own. Each goes back to a "holy root"—a moment, a conviction, or an event where something Spirit-inspired emerged to the surface and eventually caught widespread attention. In time, we came to recognize these particulars as God-given marks of our church.

How We Describe Our Totems

Here are the distinguishing marks on Fellowship Bible Church's totem pole that we consider sacred.

Living Winsome Lives

If anything drew together the initial eighteen people in 1977 for what became Fellowship Bible Church,[1] it was a desire to be the real thing. These pioneers wanted to be authentic. They didn't want to play church.

When the church called me as their pastor, I quickly embraced with them the idea that how we live is the most important thing about us. In a world made cynical from spin, images, and empty promises, "real" is convincing and compelling. It defies debate.

So I regularly preached that without a winsome lifestyle, our message of good news is lifeless (James 2:26). At issue, I emphasized, is not whether we *possess* the good news of God, but rather whether we *are* good news. "Do we incarnate the message we proclaim?" I asked.

"Real" is convincing and compelling. It defies debate.

Sometimes the answer coming back was painful.

Our city certainly didn't experience us as good news. At least, not during my first ten years of pastoring the church. We were so consumed with ourselves and our growing congregation that we all but forgot we are part of a wider community. Unfortunately, the few times our city did hear from us, it was usually in the voice of protest, over abortion, radical sex education, or obscenity.

The verbal hand grenades we occasionally threw, void of community relationships, painted us as anything but appealing. *Self-righteous* is probably the better word.

But you can't hold up winsome lifestyles as we did without this value ultimately turning its light on you and revealing what was a convicting deficiency in both our church life and witness. And it did.

This discovery led to some deep soul searching, and ultimately to a turning point. Jesus' command in Matthew 5:16 came alive to us: "Let your light shine before men in such a way that they may see your good works, and glorify your Father who is in heaven."

Jesus never just preached. He was love in action. He was out among the public connecting with people through amazing deeds that constituted a platform of credibility for his amazing claims.

Jesus' apostles followed this model of mixing amazing works with their message of amazing grace. When Peter met a lame beggar who asked for money, Peter replied, "Silver and gold have I none" (Acts 3:6, KJV), and then he healed the man in the name of Jesus Christ. The crowds were "filled with wonder and amazement" (Acts 3:10), so Peter proclaimed Jesus to them (Acts 3:12–26). If he had preached without connecting first to this man's need, the message—though still authentic—would have drawn no crowd and perhaps not even the beggar's interest.

Jesus never just preached. He was love in action.

"So, where are the works that today amaze and draw the community's interest to us and our gospel?" we asked ourselves. The answer: we didn't have any. Holding up the totem of winsome lifestyles, we challenged our people to dream of ways we could shine our light out and bless our community with amazing works. And we did.

In the months and years that followed, we turned a major corner as a leadership team and as a church. We totally changed our approach, as I explain in *The Church of Irresistible Influence.*[2]

It's now fifteen years after that pivotal turning point. Recently, I was with officials from the Arkansas prison system. They were graduating twenty prisoners from a life skill program about responsible manhood (we wrote and produced the materials). In addition, we trained the chaplain, purchased video equipment, and underwrote the costs of the program. One of the commissioners from the Department of Corrections said to me, "We thank God for your church." Hearing the commissioner's comment made me smile.

I heard the same comment just a few weeks ago after we completely refurbished a run-down Boys Club across town. One of the directors, who once was critical of our church, asked me, "Why are you doing this?" I answered, "Because the love of Christ has moved us to help those in need." He replied, "That's amazing."

This kind of community response is increasingly common for our church today, coming from a teacher whose school we remodeled, or from an inner-city agency that received a large cash gift from us with no strings attached. We're connecting with our community, and God is being glorified in the process.

Our church understands that without a compelling lifestyle, no one will listen to our life-changing message. Today, by the grace of God, we have six full-time staff working in and with our community.

Equipping Everyone to Serve

In the early days at Fellowship, when people asked, "What kind of church are you?" we came up with what was then a new term: "We're an equipping church." It meant our leaders are here to equip people to serve. The equipping-church concept, designed to summarize our niche, is based on the idea that leaders are to expend themselves in "equipping the saints for the work of service" (Ephesians 4:12). We developed this catchphrase in 1977, long before the creation of today's books that champion the term and concept.[3]

Without a compelling lifestyle, no one will listen to our life-changing message.

Our whole structure is designed to move people into various levels of service, all of which fit their gifting (1 Peter 4:10), and then celebrate when it happens. When you come to Fellowship, we don't ask *if* you will serve, but *where.* We offer hundreds of service opportunities: children's and student ministry, worship support, hospitality, community action, and more. We ask people to step into one of them the minute they step into church. More important, newcomers quickly see that the real heroes at Fellowship are the people who have found a ministry setting that uniquely matches their gifts, blessing everyone in the process.

We put a lot of effort and energy into exploring what people are good at, what motivates them, where they find the greatest fulfillment, and where those patterns can best support kingdom work. Mobilization of spiritual gifts is so important that we've created three stages to help people maximize their gifts in service to God.

Our starting point for most people is to serve with an "anywhere needed" attitude. Many approaches get the spiritual-gifts discovery process backwards by asking you, before you even start to serve, to study and discern what ministry you're supposed to have. It actually works the other way around. As Rick Warren points out, "Start serving, experimenting with different ministries, and then you'll discover your gifts. Until you're actually involved in serving, you're not going to know what you're good at."[4]

The next step then becomes the process of discovering your gifts. We call the class "Your Unique Design," and the primary intent is to help you find more fulfillment in your gift usage. It's a class we offer several times a year (we also make the supporting 250-question gift survey available at www.YourUniqueDesign.com). A majority of the adults at Fellowship have found this second step enormously helpful in understanding what specifically they have to offer and where they can be best employed in service to God's kingdom. Most of our congregation has gone through the class or to the website.

We call the third level that of a "Kingdom Builder." This level engages believers who are looking to make a greater commitment of time, effort, and money into kingdom work. They often meet in a

> The real heroes at Fellowship are the people who have found a ministry setting that uniquely matches their gifts, blessing everyone in the process.

yearlong Kingdom Builders small group. Group members think about working less in their career, perhaps giving a day or two to their church or retiring altogether from employment for kingdom work instead. Fellowship has found many of our upper-level staff that way.

I recently returned from a retreat with thirty men who are finishing a Kingdom Builders group, all in their early forties to late fifties, all successful in the marketplace. They took part in this support group because they were exploring kingdom opportunities to invest their lives in. They needed a year to think and work it through, and they needed each other to figure it out.

We believe the church is the primary place for kingdom work. We teach that whatever you do as a kingdom builder, it needs to be attached in some way to a church. That's where your support team is, cheering you on and holding you accountable, all the while moving God's church to the next level.

Barry Sorrells is a great example of this process. He and his wife, Lynda, first came to Fellowship in midlife looking for new meaning for their lives. For both, it was a time of considerable turbulence. Not long after, Barry became a Christian, got involved, took on small-group leadership, and signed up for a Your Unique Design class. He eventually joined a Kingdom Builders group to find out how he could give his work life more of a kingdom-building context.

Barry's "a-ha!" was to combine his personal background, his spiritual resources, and his work (he served as chief of staff of a large hospital here in Little Rock). "Why don't we train our doctors in some real life skills—the things I wish I had learned?" he asked. His ideas for courses were very down to earth: how to stay married while a doctor, how to use a mentor, how to handle finances, how to deal with lawsuits, and how to grow spiritually.

The head of the medical school agreed to let him offer these classes as a last-semester option. Barry recruited leading lawyers, mentor-doctors, pastors, and financial experts to teach. The experimental course got top reviews, and now the medical school has embraced the program as part of its curriculum.

Barry recently retired from active practice and now heads up this life skills program for the medical school at the University of Arkansas. Students are required to take the courses Barry has helped organize. The program also provides mentors and counseling for the students' residency years. Barry oversees it all, playing the role of a life coach. He's already receiving requests to set up the same kind of life skills program at other medical schools.

People like Barry, who find a special fit for their gifts in kingdom work, are the heroes of Fellowship.

Modeling Team Ministry

Our best and most public model of team ministry comes through team preaching. Years ago we decided to have multiple voices in our pulpit, so that each preaching pastor could also serve in other areas.

I introduced this idea of team preaching when I first came to Fellowship as pastor. I was under the conviction that everywhere you look in the New Testament you see a team. Paul appointed elders (pastors, plural) in every church he planted, and he instructed associates such as Titus to do the same. This did not mean all the pastors would be the same. Some, like Paul himself, had a gift of leadership that rallied the others. But still they operated as a team.

When I first came to Fellowship, I asked, "Why don't we have several preachers?" I had no idea how powerfully it would model teamwork to our church. The trickle-down effect on the rest of our body has been enormous.

Today we have four teaching pastors. When I stand up and play off another pastor's sermon, or when people see us go on vacation together, they catch a team spirit that infects the whole church.

The same team value characterizes our board of elders. People in other churches are always amazed to hear that we operate by unanimity on every major decision. This means every elder has to vote yes on a directional issue or else we don't move forward. If we can't reach unanimity, we pray and wait.

Yes, we've had occasional lay leaders or church staff try to build their own kingdom, functioning as a lone ranger. Eventually this is confronted in some way, by the leadership or those under the person saying, "That kind of ministry mind-set won't work here. We work together or not at all." Someone like the biblical character Diotrephes, who the Apostle John says "loves to be first among them" (3 John 9), would not do well at our church.

At Fellowship, team ministry is one of our sacred totems.

Really Doing Evangelism

A few years ago, I stood before the church and said, "One of our primary values is evangelism, and it's obvious that I've failed you. Many of you don't share your faith and are reluctant to do so. Therefore, I'm giving us an *F* as a church." I then asked the congregation for forgiveness because this was clearly an issue of leadership (remember, we're an equipping church).

In preparation for that sermon, I looked for new ways to train the church in how to invite their family and friends into a faith relationship with Jesus Christ. I know that many of our people are very good at connecting with people, even getting some to come to church with them. But they find it difficult and uncomfortable asking the person to make a faith decision.

So as I concluded my sermon, I issued a challenge: "Let's team up! I'm going to start a seekers' forum called Explore that will meet on Sunday night. For it to work, I need you who struggle with sharing your faith but are great at meeting people to go out and do what you do best: connect with spiritually searching people and bring them. I'll do what I do best: teach and explain the gospel in a friendly and engaging way. Together we will offer them a new life in Christ."

More than 150 people came to the first class. Every class since has averaged that size or greater. Our people love it! Paul Kroger is a great example of connecting. He always brings someone new to each Explore class I teach. He furnishes the relational context, selling them on the class, sitting with them, and talking with them afterward. We're a tag team: I teach, and he relates.

We've created a context that gives reluctant believers help in sharing their faith. We see the fruit of the partnership often as we baptize new believers from Explore.

Over time we've developed three levels of equipping our people to evangelize:

1. The Explore class is a hit with those who have "connecting" skills. They build relationships and bring friends, and I unfold the gospel over seven weeks in a forum that features lots of discussion and interaction.

2. We also train people who feel gifted in evangelism with a simple, seeker-friendly, evangelistic Bible study called One-To-One. This five-week interactive study is most often conducted in homes or in workplace settings. Each year we train those who enjoy engaging people with the gospel in use of this tool and send them out.

3. Our third level, the Open Forums, is done with help from Search Ministries (www.searchnational.org). The basic idea is for a small group of believers to invite their spiritually seeking friends together outside the church, usually in a home or workplace, for several sessions of open, spiritual discussion. A facilitator trained by Search Ministries guides these relaxed discussions and adds occasional comments from a Christian perspective. As people soften to the gospel, many times they go next to an Explore class or are willing to do a One-To-One study with a friend.

By the way, all of our adult evangelistic methods follow what George Barna calls "the Socratic method." That is, each is built on a high degree of interaction and questioning, as he explains in his book *Evangelism That Works*.[5]

To keep elevating the priority of evangelism, every teaching pastor has a prominent role in our evangelism ministry. The charge that "Robert Lewis doesn't practice what he preaches" isn't heard around here because every time I teach the Explore class, I draw in one or two hundred people. I also teach it in the community (currently in downtown Little Rock on Monday mornings at 7:00).

The church must never lose its heart for lost people. But it must be realistic about the kind of evangelism that really works and get church members involved. Otherwise, evangelism will continue to be the responsibility of too few people.

> The church must never lose its heart for lost people.

Building Relevance and Excellence into Everything

Martin Luther is reported to have said, "To preach the gospel at every point except where it is needed most to be heard is not to preach the gospel at all."

We constantly ask ourselves if we are hitting real needs. One simple gauge is whether people talk about it afterward. Whether a class, a worship service, or a service trip, something is wrong if there is no buzz when it's over. The only way a church can stay relevant and excellent is if we listen.

I learned years ago that the focus group is one of my best friends in church ministry. If a rightly selected group of people are asked the right questions in an open, honest environment, you get the truth about your church. In 1988 I got together a men's focus group. "How are we doing with you as men?" I asked them. Their answers surprised me. Even with all the programs and Bible studies we had for them, they felt lonely, confused, and disconnected. The message was plain and simple: our church simply wasn't meeting their needs as men.

> The only way a church can stay relevant and excellent is if we listen.

As various men tried to identify what was missing, one said, "We need something more than a Bible study. We need a place to be real and honest with one another. You know, like back in the fraternity."

On the basis of that focus group, I started an early-morning Bible study with thirty guys, called Men's Fraternity.

After a year with that group of thirty, I asked if this is what they wanted.

"Not exactly," they answered. So I listened more and (before the time when Promise Keepers hit the headlines) learned that men wanted to tackle the issues they wrestle with daily: identity issues ("who am I, and why do I feel this way?"); lingering background issues, especially with dad; loneliness issues; marriage and family issues; and more.

A light went on for me. I finally got it. Clearly, these men were expressing a deep need to find out what it means to be a man. So with their help, I created a yearlong experience called the Quest for Authentic Manhood.

I didn't realize it at the time, but I was stepping into a huge God-wave. Today, there are more than a thousand English- and Spanish-speaking Men's Fraternities across the United States (www.mens fraternity.com), including the one I still lead in Little Rock that regularly draws eight hundred to a thousand men, Wednesday mornings between September and March. All this happened because I took the time to prayerfully listen and learn what is relevant to the people I serve.

Connecting with the Community

Years ago, when we were first drawn to the idea of becoming a church of irresistible influence, we started with a huge apology. Along with a number of other like-minded churches, we called the governor, city officials, and others and made a statement of contrition, even publishing it in the newspaper. We expressed regret that we had been inwardly focused on ourselves and unconnected to them. We vowed before God that in the years to come we'd become much more externally focused on our city. In Biblical terms, you could say we ministered to the outermost parts of the world through our missions overseas, yet we ignored the call to the Jerusalem and Samaria where we lived (Acts 1:8).

As an outworking of our "listening" value, we first conducted a survey before we initiated our move into the community. We also did focus groups. Our intent was to identify needs. One of the top-ranked needs we identified in our community concerned our public schools.

We decided to create an event called ShareFest, where we would extend a helping hand to certain parts of the community, including a number of specific schools. As we approached school officials, they were at first skeptical and cautious. We assured them that our motive was not to preach but to learn how we could help them. "Would you make a wish list of things you need for your school that perhaps we could help you with?" we asked. They did, and we proceeded to bless them with all kinds of gifts: from new paint to new carpets to new playgrounds—all with no strings attached. We simply gave and left.

It worked so well we did it again the next year. On the Sunday after we completed our second year, we invited three inner-city principals to our church to speak in our Sunday worship services. As we interviewed them, each one gave glory to God for our church's investment in the community, saying, "We have a new school because of you."

Over the years, we've refurbished twenty-six schools in Little Rock, involving thousands of volunteers and hundreds of thousands of dollars. We've seen a lot of smiles come from these workdays, and also from the ongoing relationships we've established.

One of our initiatives during ShareFest is to go door-to-door, meeting people in low-income communities and asking if we can help with home repairs and needs. One day, as a member, Ray Williams, was mowing an elderly widow's yard, a young elementary school student named Michael, who lived there with his grandmother, came up to Ray and said, out of the blue, "Will you be my mentor?"

Ray's immediate thought was, *I don't have time.* Instead he asked, "What do you mean?"

The boy explained that they talk a lot at school about having a mentor, and since he really didn't have a family, he needed a mentor.

"Let me think about it," Ray answered.

God tugged at Ray's heart, and he ultimately said yes. He found out that Michael was a troubled kid. Ray asked the principal if he could start having lunch with Michael, and he received a reluctant OK. Ray started meeting Michael regularly, helping with homework, and in many ways looking out for him as a son.

Ray's entrance into that school through Michael paid off, and soon they were asking him, "Can your church send us some more mentors?" We did, and we even had the privilege of refurbishing that school through ShareFest. All because a white guy named Ray was willing to build a small bridge of love in an inner-city neighborhood.

As the scope of ShareFest has grown, we've hired staff who now work year-round exploring and implementing new ways to build bridges into our community. We call them our community strategies team, setting up ways to connect and bless the city. (The story I recounted earlier of our men's materials being used in the prison system was a result of the bridge built into the Department of Correction.)

Our next step is to take our efforts at bridge building to a much more focused level. It began after we noticed our community efforts were scattered throughout the city and lacking any coordinated effort. What if, we asked ourselves, we went to a longer strategy and set a five-to-ten-year goal to draw all our ministry efforts together in one specific area of town? What if we identify and work with neighborhood associations, churches, and schools in a concentrated way to turn a struggling area into an island of health?

Consequently we decided to unleash an initiative called Midtown Partnerships. We're adopting a 130-block area of our city, concentrating resources and people to completely reclaim a neighborhood area in a way that will startle everyone. Our hope is not just to rebuild houses but to rebuild lives inside those houses, offering tools on every level, from parenting skills to handling finances. We will work with neighborhood associations, help the schools, provide mentors, and partner with local churches to continue the work there. We want to devote intense resources to help those people become a transformed community. When we feel we've done everything we can, only then will we move on.

Multiplying Through Church Planting

A number of years ago, a group from another city began attending our church each week to worship and learn from us. They asked us to help them plant what became Fellowship Bible Church, North Little Rock.

Our goal is to find and develop young, high-capacity church leaders who want to start the kind of church that will plant other churches.

The experience became a "pillar of fire" that others noticed. Soon a group from thirty miles away came to us and made the same request. After a third group of people asked for our help in launching, we said, "Hello—something's happening!" Our elders began asking, "Is God leading us to plant churches?" Here again was something we did not seek, but the Holy Spirit led us into it. We obeyed, and it has become a major thrust of our church and a value we enthusiastically embrace.

Our church-planting investments have led to partnership with seminaries in the United States, Poland, and Guatemala. Our goal is to find and develop young, high-capacity church leaders who want to start the kind of church that will plant other churches.

We've asked God to help us plant high-impact churches. God has answered. Most of the thirty-five-plus churches we've helped plant are at least five hundred people strong, and some are two to four thousand in attendance. All but a few are growing.

The more we learned about church planting, the more we discovered that it's a great way to leverage influence. Rick Warren recently made a similar observation. He used to preach that the most important thing you can do is to lead a friend to a faith relationship with Jesus Christ. "I was wrong," he now says. We can do something even greater: "help start a church." Why? "Because a church is going to outlast you and everybody else."[6] A healthy church will continue to birth new believers—and perhaps also new churches—for generations to come.

I once said to our congregation, "God has blessed some of you with large amounts of money. Why not use it to form foundations designed to bless something your church is doing?" Three foundations have emerged so far. One couple sold the husband's company and formed a foundation that today helps underwrite Fellowship Associates, which is designed to plant churches all over America and the world. We then challenged one of our members, Steve Snider, to leave his law practice and become president of Fellowship Associates. His job now is to recruit potential church planters, bring them here, train them, release them to start their new church, and then offer consulting to help them avoid snags. We could never underwrite a year of training for several church planters, and do it year after year, without this couple being so generous with their money.

> Rick Warren says we can do something even greater than lead a friend to Jesus Christ: "help start a church."

Nor could we do it on the scale we've grown into. We've become an aggressive church-planting sponsor, planting three to seven churches a year. As I write, we are about to launch five new churches. A few months later, six new church planters will join us for their year-long leadership residency here in Little Rock.

Last summer, I flew to Spain for one of two European church plants of which we are part. In Barcelona, they're starting a Men's Fraternity and asked me to help kick it off, since one of my greatest passions is to help men discover the biblical principles of authentic manhood. From there I went to Poland, where another of our former interns is involved in church planting.

I'll never forget the visit in Poland. We went by a small church in Kraków, built during the tenth century inside the old city walls. From then until now, this city has been controlled by a long list of nations: Sweden, France, Germany, Prussia, Russia, and others. Yet despite those disruptive shifts of power you can't help but marvel at the stability and spiritual hope this church has offered through it all. I remarked to my colleagues, "Empires and nations may come and go, but God's church lasts!"

Exciting things are happening with church planting in our back yard as well. We recently helped start a church that has already crossed the two thousand mark in attendance. I remember just a few years ago when its membership was four. A hundred years from now, many of the churches we are birthing today will no doubt still be here, reaching new people for Jesus and planting scores of new churches in the process.

Praise God! That's what I want to be about. So do the people of Fellowship Bible Church.

CHAPTER

12

The Power of a
Disciplined Vision

OMETHING WAS BROKEN, BUT IT TOOK ME YEARS TO
put my finger on it.

I was a young associate pastor in a growing church in the southwestern United States. Every Monday morning, the staff met for several hours. We evaluated "last week." Then we reviewed what was coming up "this week." The senior pastor refereed as each of us came up with ideas. He decided "OK, we'll do this" or "I'd rather not do that," according to the mood of the moment.

I enjoy planning, yet I consistently left those meetings frustrated and worn out. Often I felt downright wounded. I couldn't figure out why our team meetings weren't more productive.

It was a great church to be part of. God was clearly at work. I enjoyed my fellow pastors, including our senior pastor. The things we did at staff meetings—mainly asking "What are we going to do this week?"—seemed necessary.

What, then, was the problem?

Years later, I think I have the answer. *We were making up the church's vision every Monday morning.* We were so busy detailing out and debating "this week" that we never had time to ask where our ministries were actually taking us. Meetings were often more about power plays between staff over scheduling conflicts than about hearing from staff as to how their particular ministry was advancing our overall vision and values.

Without intending it, our senior pastor had become more of a schedule-adjustment referee than a leader. He was merely holding the staff together, rarely giving vision for how our ministries could contribute to a unified movement. Big-picture issues never surfaced because we were too busy wrestling with things such as who could meet on what night or use what meeting space.

The wounded feelings came because others weren't really joining with me. Of course, I wasn't really joining into their world, either. We were all disconnected from the vision, which somehow never filtered down into our deliberations.

> We've developed a different model. We're not making up the vision each week; we're executing it.

At Fellowship, we've developed a different model.

We hardly ever have meetings like the endless ones I agonized through in my other church. Our weekly staff meeting is usually an hourlong lunch for receiving informational updates, cheering on successes, and praying for one another. Why? We're not making up the vision each week; we're executing it.

Fellowship has become the culture it is because of a *disciplined vision*, one that:

- Is shaped yearly and directed by our values
- Synchronizes with every ministry of the church
- Focuses the efforts of staff and church members
- Is clear in its scheduling and outcomes
- Inspires confidence and expectation
- Includes accountability

Later in this chapter, you'll see a chart to illustrate how this disciplined vision unfolds over the course of a year. The outcome is that we grow energized rather than exhausted, and our people are unleashed.

Disciplined vision empowers and energizes.

INTOXICATED *with* PATCHWORK VISION

I've done it, and perhaps you have too. We read about an idea or hear of a new program. It grabs our imagination. We get excited about what it can do for our church. At our next big meeting, or from the pulpit, we spontaneously announce, "This is what we're going to do!" People respond with enthusiasm.

Then Monday comes. We feel a little sheepish with ourselves for being intoxicated, or even seduced, by the idea. We begin to ponder the implications of what we announced: the time commitment, scale of mobilization, and resources needed. We muse that we might have been premature. Maybe the actual implementation now seems overwhelming. Or we become distracted by something else. Or we back off because someone voices an objection. However it happens, what started with a shout often dies a quiet death.

Know this: every time you or I let an idea die in this way, we frustrate God's people. We cause them to lose heart and doubt that the church really means what it says. We lose the congregation's trust.

Worse, we as leaders are often oblivious to the reality that we've done something wrong. But if we're constantly grabbing the latest new idea, moving from one quick fix to the next, danger signals should light up all over our dashboard. Why? If this is your pattern, you have a serious problem. I call it a "vision vacuum."

Initially at Fellowship Bible Church, I did this very thing. I remember one year in particular, my fifth at the church. Attendance had grown by hundreds that year. We were reeling with the implications, while also trying to discover where God wanted us to go next. We knew it was important to give vision during our growth, but we never seemed to have time for making sense of it all. The big picture was missing.

At the time, we had three pastors on staff. One of us would get excited about something, tell the others, and get a program going. The other two of us did likewise, applying quick fixes right and left. It was chaotic and confusing. We were looking for answers, but without a unifying vision to tie it all together. We regularly came up short.

In cases like this, any new idea often amounts to little more than patchwork over a wound. For instance, suppose your church's small groups aren't working. You look around, hear that Willow Creek is doing something great with small groups, buy a book about it, and next Sunday announce the new plan.

This is not a vision that will unleash power. It's merely a patch for something broken. There's a big difference between a quick fix to stop the bleeding, and a well-thought-through vision that takes the values you hold as sacred to the next level.

Quick fixes and patchwork programs without thoughtful deliberation make up what I call an outside-in approach. You're borrowing programs from the outside as a substitute for the deeper work that needs addressing: vision that establishes your culture.

You can also have the world's greatest written mission statement, but it's no more than words on paper if it's not synchronized with the actual values and activity of the whole. In fact, a pattern of patchwork fixes—"vision of the moment" announcements—actually does more harm than good, as the congregation senses these new ideas are disconnected and have no tie to any whole. Such moments cause the congregation to become cynical or distrusting, recognizing that you haven't taken time to determine and work out the Holy Spirit's course for the church.

I'm not criticizing the practice of adapting great ideas from other churches. We do so at times here. But there's a more disciplined way to adapt a new idea. Suppose, modifying the same example, your church's small groups

> A new idea often amounts to little more than patchwork over a wound, not a vision that will unleash power.

aren't working and you hear that Willow Creek is having great success with their small groups. Instead of immediately making a grand announcement that fizzles the next week, what if you first explore how small groups fit into the unique mission and vision, and the values of the church? You then bring the discussion to a leadership team, who talk and pray with you about how to adapt the idea so that it brims with the culture of your specific locality. You talk through the specific details of this new venture with your staff and lay leaders, working out specific details. Only then do you announce it publicly as a go.

If vision is going to be unleashed from the inside out, processing the vision together must become a value that's deeply inculcated in leadership and staff.

STARTING *with the* PURPOSES *of* GOD

The early church noticed that King David, who led Israel into its greatest era, "served the purposes of God in his own generation" (Acts 13:36). David's long-range vision for Israel was the purpose of God for his time.

The church is at its best when it serves the mission of God, not some lesser objectives.

But how do you discover God's desire for your church? I believe there are two answers. First, God gives visionary or directional leaders to the church (often the senior pastor or senior leadership team) to discern God's unique direction for a particular body of believers.

> Processing the vision together must become a value that's deeply inculcated in leadership and staff.

In the healthiest churches I know, if you ask "Who's the vision caster?" there's an immediate answer. Even if a church moves to intentional team ministry, it does not want multiple, conflicting visions. The best churches are team ministries *with* a vision caster.

The visioning task is mystical. Leaders made of flesh and clay (see 2 Corinthians 4) must take the time to connect with the Holy Spirit, translating those encounters into pathways for how the church can best serve the purposes of God. Integrity and humility are the primary safeguards for one who is gifted in this way.

Second, the purposes of God come right out of Scripture. This is always the best starting point as the Holy Spirit teaches a church its unique values for a unique locale. For instance, one of the specific purposes of God for every church is in presenting the gospel aggressively to its community (Matthew 28:18–20). We don't need a new revelation from God to know that. So the purposes of God are made known for the church through gifted visionaries and Holy Scripture.

ANNUAL CYCLE *of* VISION

For Fellowship, the rhythm of disciplined vision is an annual one. It starts with the recognition that the long-range vision for our church is our values—our totem pole. The vision for the coming months is simply how we're going to rightly implement those values. These outcomes are the practical how-to's of connecting our people's hearts and actions back to our values.

> The long-range vision for each church is its values.

We changed to an annual cycle because of those chaotic growth years when we were recreating the vision weekly. We were all becoming burned out and frustrated, so we enlisted the help of a consultant, Bobb Biehl (www.MasterPlanningGroup.com). He gave us this strategic wisdom: "You need a process that allows the vision God gives you to be personally embraced by your staff and by your congregation."

Bobb's advice helped us find a pattern for doing that. First, I realized the importance of being able to say, "As your pastor, I've spent time in prayer and reflection, and I sense this is where God is leading Fellowship." To do so, I had to discipline my time. I started getting away from the church during January, spending time alone with God, trying to craft the first edges of a vision—where we should go and what we should be doing.

Then I brought these "visions" back to our leadership, putting them in front of the elders for interaction and polishing. They enjoy this sense of vision ownership as it becomes not *my* vision but *our* vision.

After that, it goes through a process by which the vision is shared by the staff. This usually takes all spring, requiring much discussion and understanding. We work out the specific implications on job descriptions, budgets, and calendars. We ask the elders to review it one more time. Ultimately we bring the shared vision to the congregation as a more completed, well-thought-out way than I could ever achieve alone.

Sometimes I'm asked, "What if blockers and people with an alternate agenda try to thwart your leadership?" As a visionary leader I must remember that not every vision going through my mind is from God. So I don't mind submitting it to others. If what I've heard is from God, it will ultimately come to pass. Yes, some people who interact with the vision have missed the voice of God, intentionally or otherwise. Yet the visionary leader has to believe; as someone said of the early church, "If it be of God, ye cannot overthrow it" (Acts 5:39). If I've received a vision from God, unique to this locale, it will stand up to scrutiny. It will win the hearts of people because God will go before me. I have to believe that I'll see God work it out in our midst, confirming that it really is from God.

Our best Sunday each year is the state-of-the-church address. The experience of that day unleashes an unbelievable unity, passion, and energy in our church.

The most common feedback from the congregation is, "Wow! I can't believe our church is going to do this. I'm so excited about what we're doing." Then they say, "How can I help?" That's honestly how most people respond every year. Next, our staff, who have been working on the plans over the summer, go immediately into execution phase.

A few people push us to see if we've thought everything through, or they question whether we're doing the best job of prioritizing the budget. Their motive is usually to discern if we mean what we say;

have we done our homework? We're certainly open to interactions like that, in case someone shows us something we've missed. Frankly, it's rare that anyone finds a major oversight.

The August 2003 vision message illustrates the power of a vision that's been disciplined before it goes public. In my message that Sunday, I announced several huge changes. I explained that we were dramatically revising our small-group system, adding new worship venues, altering our Sunday schedule, and elevating one of the pastors to become the new directional leader of Fellowship. This radical vision neither backfired nor caused mass anxiety. Instead, it was embraced; people applauded what they believed God was doing in their church.

The next week, we went from three services to six (some were "video venues"), and we never missed a beat. In fact, people brought their friends, confident that the changes would be a good experience. Why? In part, because they know that our vision is not something that dribbles over the pulpit and gets swept away the next day by the cleaning crew. They have confidence that we've prayed, spiritually discerned, and carefully planned. They trust that we'll be successful in implementation.

A man who has been part of Fellowship for years drew me aside and said, "Sometimes you announce stuff I don't like, but I can't argue with results. You get it done. You guys do what you say."

I replied affirmatively, because over the years this disciplined process has been blessed by God.

One of our models is Acts 15, where the Jerusalem council is wrestling over sensitive issues associated with the future of the first-century church. In that passage, you don't see one person as the source of all the answers. You do see Peter and James cast vision, but then the whole group of apostles and elders wrestles with their ideas. Ultimately they write down their decision, stating "it seemed good to the Holy Spirit and to us" (Acts 15:28). That's disciplined vision.

By the time we get to our annual state-of-the-church address, we have that same conviction: "We believe God is leading us to do this,

this, and this." A disciplined vision is well thought out, prayed over, and shaped within relationships of godly, gifted people.

One of my statements in the August 2003 vision message was a major one for me personally. I announced the elders' decision, with my blessing and recommendation, that Tim Lundy would be appointed as the new directional leader for our church. He is replacing me after twenty-three years in that job. It was a move we all knew in our hearts God wanted for Tim and for me. I am going on to pioneer new things through our church while supporting Tim as he adjusts to his new leadership role.

> A disciplined vision is well thought out, prayed over, and shaped within relationships of godly, gifted people.

In January 2004, Tim and I went away together as two visionaries. We spent time alone and together, seeking God and dreaming. We energized each another in conversation. I helped him produce and craft his first pass at where he senses God is leading our church in the months ahead. Ultimately, Tim brought back a draft form of our next steps, just as I've done for many years. He then led the process of asking our elders to add color. Next he walked the staff through it, continuing the cycle depicted in the (abbreviated) chart on the following page.

There are many ways to shape vision in a context of unity and community. Leaders who are perhaps more spontaneous than I am might work through circles of relationships. Rather than formally charting out the process, the leader continually talks through various visions with top staff, relationally working to achieve buy-in, doing the same with the church board and other levels of staff, and finally presenting it to the congregation, inviting them into it.

Whatever your personality or particular method, remember that God blesses vision that promotes unity and community. It's a supernatural thing when unity develops. "How wonderful it is, how pleasant, for God's people to live together in harmony!" (Psalm 133:1, GNT).

Church Planning:
How Fellowship Bible Church Discerns What the Holy Spirit Is Trying to Do

	January	February	March	April	May	August	Next 12 months
What?	Vision casting	Shaping and Unifying	Focusing	Refining	Approving	Announcing	Executing
Who?	Church's visionary leader	Elders and leadership team	Elders, leadership team, staff	Staff	Elders, leadership team, staff	Church's visionary leader	Staff / Congregation
Place?	Retreat setting	Board room	Various meetings	Individual planning	Staff meetings with appropriate leaders	"State of the Church" worship services	Throughout the church body
Outcome?	First vision	Unified vision	Unified vision	Staff plans, first draft	Staff plans, approved version	Congregational clarity, understanding and vision	Effective and unifying ministry blessed by God

ANSWERING *the* WHY QUESTION

Real vision answers both the *why* and the *what*. It captures people's imagination with what we're going to do and why we're going to do it.

Of the two, *why* is more important. Unfortunately, most church leaders equate vision with a focus on results, so they spend more time talking about the *what*. I believe this is a mistake.

Addressing the *why* question touches both head and heart. Insights as to *why* connect back to values and also touch people's emotions.

Real vision tells us why this is so important, why it should be a priority, why it matters, and why we should feel and embrace it so strongly. *Why* goes to the heart. It helps people work through their philosophical roadblocks even more than it promises the results of the vision. If I don't answer the *why*, people may go along, but they'll do so without passion. If you and I successfully speak to the *why* question and people buy in, they'll be self-starters.

Once I'm done, if I've addressed the right questions of the heart, everyone should be able to say, "I can do that!" Real vision helps people work through fears and other questions of the heart, even more than it promises the results of the vision.

> Unfortunately, most church leaders spend more time talking about the *what* than the *why*.

For several years our church has sponsored a national leadership conference (www.fellowshipassociates.com). One of the workshops that usually fills first deals with vision and strategic planning. Our learning is that many churches are making up their vision moment by moment. It is a habit that regularly undercuts a church's effectiveness. People become frustrated when their leaders espouse a new vision every month.

It's not just vision but disciplined vision that engages, empowers, and energizes. Through it, you're pointing people to the horizon, and on the horizon they'll see an exciting vision they can embrace, believe in, and (most important) trust God for.

Learning to Spot Opportunity

WHAT IS YOUR WAY OF FINDING OUT THE NEEDS OF people in your church and in your community? In most cases, you don't know what's really going on in their minds and hearts unless you create some intentional lines of discovery. Until you do so, it is easy to miss the most important needs, which may be right in front of you.

The more you know about your church and community, the more you'll be able to discern what God wants you to do next. This simple notion has enabled Fellowship Bible Church to dramatically increase its effectiveness in ministry over the years.

I'm a big advocate of leadership that stays connected at the grassroots level. Whenever I've been disconnected from happenings in the trenches of people's lives, I've missed an opportunity for God to shape our church and move it along certain spiritual lines. It's not always easy to open our eyes to certain developments right in front of us, things that are so obvious that we miss them. This is why increasing our *objective* awareness is vital to making space for vision, creativity, and leadership.

LISTENING *and* BUILDING AWARENESS

The pitfall of most church leadership is that many of its decisions don't come from reflection on good intelligence the leaders have scouted out; instead, they are reactive or made on the fly. Shepherds need to know the condition of their flock. The Bible says, "Know well the condition of your flocks, and pay attention to your herds" (Proverbs 27:23).

In most cases, we need help from listening and building objective awareness. The simplest listening point is to hang out with people who are on the front lines of ministry. For us pastors, this happens naturally when we initially come to a church or when we serve a church that doesn't have many paid staff. As long as the pastor has open ears and is looking for clues about what God wants to bless, then informal "How is this ministry working for you?" conversations can uncover many important spiritual insights of where God is and isn't moving.

> The simplest listening point is to hang out with people who are on the front lines of ministry.

Most pastors don't realize that a lot of the Holy Spirit's signals are communicated through these interactions. Pastors can discover rich opportunities and better focus ministry activity from these close-range interactions.

Blind spots begin occurring when pastors isolate themselves in their office or depend on conversations with staff about what the staff *think* people are experiencing. At times I've found their reports to be only half the story. As a result, key insights, potential trouble spots, and strategic opportunities pass by without anyone ever noticing.

Church growth can also be problematic to good information gathering. It can push ministry leaders into management assignments and away from people, removing them from the very dynamic that was opening doors of opportunity in the first place. They may think they can still obtain the perspective they need by reading ministry reports or by getting an assistant's or another staff member's perspective about a problem. These things may help, but nothing can substitute adequately for direct contact with the everyday lives of people who are wrestling with the various pressures they feel from the world around them, or for getting their take on any ministries they're involved with through the church. This reality cannot be emphasized enough.

How I Unintentionally Stopped Listening

We fell into the blind spot of no longer listening at Fellowship, and to this day I still feel some of the bruises. During my initial years with the church, we experienced quick growth. Much of it came through the outreach of well-developed lay leaders who had fairly solid spiritual lives. I was in close touch with them because I was discipling many of them through various teams and classes. As a result, when I preached I spoke knowingly to their spiritual level, with their spiritual experiences in mind. I approached my sermons with a clear sense of connection with our entire congregation. I felt I "knew well the condition of my flock."

Nothing can substitute for direct contact with the everyday lives of people or getting their take on ministries they're involved with.

Unfortunately, as the church grew, I let myself become more removed from the street-level spiritual dialogue of both newcomers and long-term church members. As I kept preaching with this new disconnect, I began to receive feedback that my messages were less effective. I couldn't figure out why.

Then I began to teach a newcomer's class called Discovery. As I interacted firsthand with people's questions, I discovered that my preaching was way over their heads. I found I was assuming too much. My pulpit language was peppered with a great deal of insider church language they couldn't grasp. This group, which typified a lot of our recent growth, was still working through many of the basic concepts about the gospel, forgiveness, and walking in the Spirit. I also discovered that I was out of touch with the pain they struggled with, and out of touch with the help they wanted my preaching to provide.

Worse, I learned that certain ministry programs of our church, such as our small-group ministry, were missing the mark as well. As I regained firsthand access to our people, I was dismayed to find out that a number of the problems with our small groups had been going on for some time. The problems were so significant, in fact, that we eventually concluded our whole small-group system was no longer effective. I discovered all this as a leader simply by getting some serious face time with our newcomers.

The next chapter explains what happened in more detail. The gist is that what we, as leaders, thought was encouraging people was in many ways actually holding them and us back as a church. We initially built our small-group system to address our needs for community, spiritual life development, and strengthening marriages. By God's grace, many of our people achieved success in those areas and were now asking, "What else can we do?" They wanted to explore a new level of spiritual adventure and service in giving their lives away for Christ, but our structure was saying, "You need to keep repeating seventh grade." They didn't want to keep going over the same kind of material we were offering without any new opportunity for spiritual adventure. But because we hadn't gone to their groups and put our ear to the floor, we missed it. We didn't know how to spot failure or new opportunity because we didn't take the time to really listen. We assumed way too much.

> People wanted to go to a new level of giving their lives away for Christ, but our structure held them back because we didn't take the time to listen.

After we learned the condition of our flock, we did away with our existing small-group system and offered more of a staged approach. Newcomers got the foundational material, but then later as they mastered these concepts they could move into a number of options: works of service, alternate study topics, and applied experiences such as evangelism and discipleship. As we provided these responses to our people's needs, we saw a pent-up pressure being released that led to immediate numerical growth, a heightened sense of excitement, more noticeable satisfaction, and a new spiritual level that we hadn't even imagined.

LISTENING, LEARNING, *and* BEING SURPRISED

The same informal listening approach that we took inside the church also worked for helping us reach out more meaningfully to our city. In Chapter Eleven, I describe how engaged we are today with our community. Long ago, my main civic involvement was to express disappointment in how our community was departing from its Christian moorings. Rather than dialoguing, I reacted, assuming that we needed to correct our community by using strong, hostile denunciations, throwing these fireballs over the walls of the church into the community. Predictably, many in our city came to view us as people who believed themselves to be above the community and self-appointed to speak down to it. For my part, I assumed that if I actually tried to initiate some form of dialogue with our city, they'd say, "We don't want anything to do with you. Leave us alone."

Some of our staff said, "Let's go and meet our neighbors." We discovered that our assumptions were dead wrong.

I couldn't have been more wrong, but I had no awareness because I never took any tangible steps to find out. I acted merely on personal assumptions.

In the late 1980s and early 1990s, some of our staff said, "Let's go and meet our neighbors. Let's talk to our community and hear from them." We then launched a series of initiatives where we interacted with other churches first and spoke with city officials and then with community people. We asked, "What do you think our church could do to make a positive difference in the city?" and "How can we help you?"

What we heard was humbling. We discovered that our assumptions were dead wrong. Most people's "Great, let's talk" reaction absolutely shocked us. They were genuinely interested in partnering with us! We saw this attitude in other churches as well as in community leaders.

It continues to this day, by the way. Churches tend to collaborate with us more as kingdom builders rather than as turf competitors, probably because we all take the view that the needs are so great and the opportunities so many that there's always room for someone else to come and help. We've built relationships with city officials, schools, neighborhood associations, nonprofits, and community leaders. If we ask their help, they usually respond quickly to us—and we do likewise for them.

Back when our dialogue first started, we also did some research on the spiritual dynamics of our community. We learned that it isn't as Christian or churchgoing as we previously thought. In fact, we were stunned to find that even here in America's supposed Bible belt, our community is below the average in church attendance; it was eye-opening. We were thinking, for instance, that most of our neighbors were churched, but then we learned that barely 40 percent of Arkansans in the Little Rock area go to church.[1]

We were also wrong in how the community perceived the church. We learned that the public schools had a negative feeling toward churches like ours, seeing us as organizations that triggered white flight (which, quite frankly, has some truth to it). Over time, however, as we reach out to our public schools this negative attitude has significantly been reduced. Our desire to genuinely serve our public schools has led to warm, positive, and ongoing relationships.

After initially discovering that we were clueless about certain spiritual needs in our community, we've come a long way. We've learned that on almost any initiative we can build a bridge to other churches and to other centers of community influence simply by humbling ourselves and saying, "How can we work together?"

Our increased knowledge of the community has led to some unbelievable ministry achievements and church-community partnerships. You can read about many of them in detail in my book *The Church of Irresistible Influence*. In recent years we've even had to say, "Look at all the potential bridges we can now cross into our community; which is best? Which are the most strategic, because we can't do them all?" This is incredible progress when you consider just a few years ago there were no bridges at all for our church to connect with our city.

USING TOOLS *to* INCREASE AWARENESS

In many churches, attendance outstrips the church leaders' ability to know everyone or for everyone to know each other. When that happens, artificial bridges of communication must be established for keeping up with people. I tell people at our conferences, "A bridge is an unnatural connection. It's unnatural to cross a large river, for example. But once you create this unnatural connection, it allows previously impossible opportunities of communication to take place."

The bridge analogy has led our church to discover "artificial bridges" that increase our understanding and awareness. The best one is the focus group. It's an informal, one-time gathering of six to twelve people who discuss and comment, from personal experience, on the topic we want to learn about. Focus-group research involves organized discussion with good listening on the leader's part.

Some people are professionally trained as focus-group facilitators, and we've occasionally used them with good success. Most of the time, however, what we call focus groups are simply informal sessions that involve bringing people together, asking hard questions we need answered, and listening carefully without being defensive.

Let's say we were struggling with how to do a better job of reaching young women. We create a focus group of young women, both in the church and in the community. We then ask several simple questions, such as "What are the needs you're feeling as a woman?" and "Where is our church missing an opportunity to serve and spiritually assist people like you?" Out of the discussion comes awareness that helps us spot opportunity. On the basis of what we learn, we're better able to create or refine various ministry vehicles.

When we do focus groups, I usually try to include a few people I call "key ministry indicators." These are people who love the church, have great insights and instincts, and are also highly engaged in the community or marketplace. They know we appreciate them. We also know they will be brutally honest with us if we ask them. If we're not meeting the needs of the group they represent, we know they'll tell us. All we need to do is to ask and then genuinely listen.

Warning: if you do focus groups, you'll hear some things that hurt. You may think you have a great ministry in a certain area, and then the first three people to speak tell you how they think the ministry falls short. Some of us feel as though we're on the witness stand in the movie *A Few Good Men,* when Jack Nicholson (Col. Nathan Jessup) prods Tom Cruise (Lt. Daniel Kaffee): "You can't handle the truth." But we need to hear the truth. The Bible says, "Faithful are the wounds of a friend" (Proverbs 27:6).

Remember that a focus group doesn't speak absolute truth. The participants may even debate one another. You're looking for the two or three things that stand out, that almost everyone agrees with. The group may not offer answers, but if they can pinpoint a genuine problem, blind spot, or missed opportunity then you're halfway to an answer that might open up wonderful new doors.

If you're so defensive that you can't hear what might come across as criticism, then you've got a bigger issue: a heart problem, a denial problem, or a pride problem. It's OK if you don't know what to do, but if you don't *want* to know what's really going on, your focus is not that of one who serves. It's something else.

> It's OK if you don't know what to do, but if you don't *want* to know what's really going on, you have a heart problem.

Sometimes it takes several rounds of feedback to figure out a solution, as I describe in Chapter Eleven with our men's ministry. I was offering them the only thing I knew to do: a Bible study. It took two years of noodling with thirty to forty guys until we came to clarity. I finally learned that they wanted to go on a quest for authentic manhood. Instead of Bible study front and center, we learned to start with the struggles men feel first, and then on the backside we brought in the Bible for answers.

This different approach had amazing results. For two years we had a Bible study with thirty men. In the third year we changed our approach, announcing that the subject would be manhood, and that part of our time would be spent in small groups. I remember driving up to the church building and finding three hundred guys there. I said aloud, "That's it!" As soon as the meeting was over. I phoned one of our staff. "I've found it!" I shouted. "The issue is manhood! They want to figure out what it means to be a man—that's the need!" Using the Scripture to facilitate meeting the need was easy after I discovered what the men were really hungering for.

In fact, this discovery helped me learn a whole new approach to communication for all ages. Even in my preaching, they like me to address hard-edged needs up front, and then show how the Bible solves it. Shape the issue first, and then let the Bible speak. I used to start by talking about what the Bible says about fear, for instance, and at the end say, "Now let's address some of the fears you face." Now I ask, "How many of you feel afraid? Maybe it's because someone offered you a job that you felt was too big. Or maybe it's because you are in a relationship that you fear will fall apart if you're truly honest and authentic with that person." Once I get people identifying and feeling their fears, only then do I show them what the Bible says is the solution. Real-life needs are always up front.

In addition to conducting focus groups, we take all kinds of surveys. Appendix One in this book contains excerpts from one of our periodic church surveys, where we ask the congregation to evaluate and rate all aspects of our worship services. We ask about our sermons, "Are they hitting the right topics? Do they go too long?" We ask about our worship times, "Do you like the style of music? Is it too contemporary?" We ask about our dramas, "Do they add to our worship?" We ask if we pray enough. We ask if we're using technology appropriately.

Every bulletin has a feedback form on it. We also offer a first-impressions card to first-time guests (an example is given on the following page). We do occasional research projects in the community. We go on what I call regular scouting missions, where we send an elder or senior staff member out to attend a group or meeting, and then provide us with firsthand observations.

Our people know that we may address an issue and fail, but at least they know we tried to do everything we could to understand it. They know that Fellowship is a church always trying to find God's best for its people. Part (and it's only a part) of this understanding starts with as much honest, objective feedback as we can get.

First-Impression Postcard

Our church wants to serve you better. Please take a moment to give us your initial impressions of your time with us:

• What did you notice first? _____
• What did you like best? _____
• What did you like least? _____
• What caused you to visit our church? _____

Thanks so much for this valuable feedback.
Tim Lundy, Teaching Pastor

(adapted from Fellowship Bible Church, Little Rock, Arkansas)

FEEDBACK *from* CHRONIC GRUMPS

Do we listen to everyone's feedback? Yes and no. It's easy to identify feedback comments that come from the kind of person Gordon Mac-Donald calls a VDP: a very draining person.[2] This is someone who always has an axe to grind and who feels we're never good enough. Those comments are rarely constructive or helpful.

Instead, I especially want to hear from healthy people—the growing ones. There are certain people in our church about whom I know that if they're happy, the whole church is happy. They represent the kind of people we'd never want to lose: those whose lives are growing and bearing fruit, who do the most effective ministry, and who have the greatest impact in the long run. By listening to them, our church can gain rich insights into how God is moving and which items of ministry are working best.

An added benefit of surveying healthy people is the chance to catch frustration before it grows too big. If they say, "You know, I'm starting to get concerned about our student ministry," then I've learned it's time to move into action to know more. I don't want to hear about it after they've left Fellowship and joined another church because their kids gave up on our youth group and joined one somewhere else. If we lose people like that, it's because we aren't listening. It's a failure of leadership.

> I especially want to hear from healthy people—the growing ones. They represent the kind of people we'd never want to lose.

Take Time Away *to* Reflect *and* Create

As a leader, your personality may be that of an opportunity person, a goal setter, or a problem solver. But you can be *none* of these effectively if you don't have awareness and information. An awareness approach energizes all three of those leadership styles. I can't solve a problem I don't fully know about, and I can't spot an opportunity if I don't know what's really going on.

As we gain new awareness at Fellowship, we process this information with key people. We try to do so before it's at crisis level. We intentionally make time to get away, reflect, and create. When I was the church's directional leader, I regularly took a week away every year to prayerfully examine the next steps for our vision as a church. Others, both staff and lay leaders, follow this model on a smaller scale.

When church leaders begin sensing that something is amiss, their typical response (if they're not careful) is to work harder, do more, or upgrade their programming by depending on a faddish solution to solve the still-unidentified real need. They may even respond by telling the people of the church, "The problem is that you need to be more committed." Sadly, reactions of this sort don't address the root problem of not knowing where people really are in their thoughts and hearts. You've got to know before you do.

Most church leaders waste a lot of time, effort, and energy unless we're entirely intentional about learning how to listen.

Perhaps there are a few church leaders who can skip an objective learning process. They have a unique, intuitive gift of sensing what to do. People like that, however, are few in number.

Most church leaders (including myself) waste a lot of time, effort, and energy unless we're entirely intentional about learning how to listen. This involves taking time to increase our awareness—sometimes even conducting focus groups, or obtaining specialized research, or having discussions with key people both inside and outside our church. Only after such listening moments do we look to God and each other as leaders for a new direction.

ALTERNATIVE *to a* PLUG-*and*-PLAY APPROACH

Sometimes you don't know what to do even after you have listened or received helpful feedback. You have rightly defined the issue for your locale, but you don't have a workable solution for it. You need something to meet the need, but you simply don't have time or knowledge or appropriate skills to create the resources or approach to meet it. If you do know clearly what your target is, then it is entirely appropriate to hunt for whatever best practices you can find somewhere else that are helpful in addressing it. This approach is different from an obsession with the latest, greatest program. With this approach, you find (and perhaps tailor) something that God has blessed somewhere else in order to meet a need or opportunity in a particular spot that you as a leader know the Holy Spirit wants you to address.

This kind of situation is what led us to our Open Forums, which Search Ministries already had in place (as I describe in Chapter

Eleven). A lot of people had told us that their unchurched friends weren't ready to jump into discussion of the gospel, but they were willing to talk about spiritual things in a question-and-answer format. Their biggest need was for a safe place where they could be with people they knew and respected. They weren't ready to feel the pressure of a church yet, for a variety of reasons.

In short, we discovered an open door of spiritual opportunity, but we didn't have an answer for it. So we said, "Let's look for someone else's best practices to solve our problem." After asking around, we found Search Ministries. Their open-forum approach to inquisitive seekers seemed like a good solution for our situation, so we tried it to meet the opportunity we had uncovered. It proved to be a perfect fit.

Likewise, at one point many of our small groups were being drained by needy people. Our leaders gave us feedback that certain people with addictions were bleeding the life out of their groups. They'd start talking about their issue, and then the group would become refocused into a therapeutic group, entirely wrapped up in helping the addicted. As this problematic issue worked its way through various lay leaders and staff who oversee our small-group ministry, each of them told us, "We can't solve it." So we went out and found a solution.

We customized the Celebrate Recovery program from Saddleback to meet this specific need. Today, if someone has an ongoing habit, addiction, or problem that begins to overwhelm a particular small group, we stop it, but in a constructive way. We offer them the better opportunity of Celebrate Recovery, which functions as a partner with our small groups. It has worked beautifully for us.

What is God doing elsewhere? Which best practices is he blessing? It doesn't have to be new; it simply has to produce the results we have discovered we need by listening. Borrowed programs such as Open Forums and Celebrate Recovery have really upgraded a number of our ministry efforts at Fellowship. Instead of importing plug-and-play programs or patching up something that's failing, they have helped us respond to vital ministry opportunities that we uncovered through listening.

KEEP TOTEMS FRONT *and* CENTER

This chapter is about spotting opportunities in the church. In it we emphasize what we've learned at Fellowship about asking good questions, listening, reflecting, and prayerfully finding solutions. We strongly believe that the more we know, the more we will know what to do.

> The more we know, the more we will know what to do.

But something else bears mention here that is just as important. Whenever we survey any aspects of ministry at Fellowship, we also review them in the light of our totems. Our totems filter and measure the value of each ministry we are involved in as a church, regardless of how people feel about them. So in every ministry we ask these kingdom questions:

- Are we winning people to Jesus Christ?
- Are we making disciples of Jesus Christ?
- Are people genuinely embracing and living out the Christian life?

On the one hand, we as leaders are always actively seeking to spot opportunity. On the other hand, in whatever we do, we never want to stray from our totems, our core values.

Both are necessary for culture-rich churches and the high-impact ministries that flow from them.

14

Courageous Adjustments to Safeguard the Values

Y OU HAVE ONLY TWENTY-FIVE BASKETBALL GAMES left in those knees," the bone specialist said to me in an uncomfortably serious tone. He then gave me two choices: stay on my present path and have problems, or make a major adjustment.

It was hard to believe the X rays my orthopedist was showing me in his downtown Little Rock office. Until recent months I'd never had pain in my knees, but, as he pointed out, I didn't have much cartilage left. "You're just a small fraction away from being bone-on-bone," he said.

I could live without basketball. Jogging would be much harder to give up. I'd been a jogger most of my life. "You've got to make a decision to look for alternative forms of exercise," the doctor continued. "If you keep jogging, you'll need a knee replacement within ten years."

Although his words hit me hard, I heeded my orthopedist's advice. I bought an elliptical trainer (which is far easier on joints than a treadmill), and have run vigorously on it for some time now. I had an X ray recently, and the miniscule amount of cartilage is still there. I have no pain in my knees because I was willing to make adjustments in order to safeguard a higher value: not my jogging, but my health.

A college buddy who played on the football team with me experienced his first knee pains about the same time as I did. He received the same orthopedic warning, but he didn't change his ways. A few years later, he had a knee-replacement operation. Today he still walks with a certain amount of pain.

Life itself teaches the importance of making constant adjustments, as I had to do personally if I wanted to stay fit. Fellowship Bible Church has likewise had to make courageous changes all its life, as a way of safeguarding our values as a congregation.

Contrary to the stereotype, adjustments and values go hand in hand.

Valuing Community, But *in* Ever-Adapting Forms

Our values at Fellowship include relevance, community, evangelism, and discipleship. Over the years, we've had to make some courageous decisions to keep following them.

Consider our value of community. In 1977, Fellowship was one of the first churches around that went completely to a small-group approach for its spiritual formation. Back in 1977, it was really unusual for a thriving church not to have Sunday school. Instead, our congregation, birthed originally from Gene Getz's Fellowship Bible Church in Dallas, used the minichurch idea he developed,[1] with one elder overseeing every thirty or so people. The minichurches met in homes, with the elder shepherding and instructing. This was the foundation on which the church's sense of community was initially built.

> Our church has had to make courageous changes all its life, as a way of safeguarding our values.

When I came as pastor in 1980, the minichurch system was stagnating. We couldn't produce elders fast enough. The size of thirty didn't work, either. I had just finished my doctorate on the topic of small-group formation and learned that no one can build or sustain high-quality, intimate community with thirty people. The better groups tended to be in the range of ten to twelve.

People at that time were nervous about making any changes to the model since Gene was so highly respected (he remains, by the way, our longtime friend and advisor). Yet we took the courageous step of scrapping the thirty-person small-group program and dramatically downsizing to groups of ten to twelve maximum. We changed the name from minichurch to community group. We no longer placed an elder over each group; rather, we used lay leaders with strong social skills. We trained them to facilitate the lessons. The model became a discipleship program for small-group leaders, where they would go "practice" their discipleship with their small groups. We followed a uniform approach, with an accompanying uniform curriculum.

Over the next ten years, we brought a lot of people into maturity through leadership training and small-group leadership experiences. Soon healthy, mature laypeople with pastoral skills were circulating throughout the body life of Fellowship Bible Church. They became our leaders. In the process we fostered a strong sense of community among the majority of the congregation.

Ten years later, in 1990, we took a survey. Our intent was to get a good feel for how we were doing in our value of community. One startling finding was that people who had been in our small-group system for more than five years were losing interest in their group and were often becoming discouraged. They said our small groups didn't feel challenging enough; they weren't getting a chance to build deeper community because we shuffled the groups too often. The Bible material also seemed too light. "It's community group 'lite,' and not challenging enough," many said. "We need more options and opportunities," others said. "We feel stuck here." Those frustrations led many to become increasingly disenchanted and question the value of small-group involvement altogether.

> We brought a lot of people into maturity through leadership training and small-group leadership experiences.

We formed a number of focus groups and found additional confirmation in what the surveys had revealed.

So in 1990 we scrapped our small-group system—again. This time we moved to something with more options. The new approach initially grouped people by the season of life they were in. The focus of season-of-life groups was on building strong relational connections and growing together in the Christian life. Then, after connecting for three years with others in their season of life, members could move into a ministry-based system known as Common Cause. In these small groups, people came together because of common ministry interests (students, missions, discipleship, social action, and so on) that they were passionate about. These groups still met regularly to pray and study God's Word together, but unlike season-of-life groups they also added the doing of specific kinds of ministry together. It was this common ministry focus that was at the core of all Common Cause groups.

Almost overnight with these changes, our small-group system revitalized. Participation increased dramatically too. So did the enthusiasm.

Then, thirteen years later, we realized this small-group system had run its course as well. Why? Members told us it didn't provide enough meeting times or enough ministry options. People wanted to do more activities together. They wanted to meet not on the current pattern of every other week for the entire year, but for about six straight weeks back-to-back, followed by several weeks off to have time for a mission trip, retreat, service project, or other personal interest. Additionally, they wanted more mobility in being able to change groups. As before, we did interviews to confirm what wasn't working and to discern what would fit best for today.

For more than thirty years, the value of community has remained constant. Perpetuation of the small-group *structure* is not important.

In 2003, we scrapped our small-group system a third time and introduced a new small-group approach based on multiple ministry options. We're still working out bugs as this book goes to press, but clearly it has revitalized us again.

For more than thirty years, the value has remained constant: people need the kind of biblical community that helps them build relationships and grow spiritually. The small-group structure itself is secondary. It's not sacred, or even important, to perpetuate the structure; what's sacred is biblical community. All along the way, we have made courageous adjustments to safeguard this kingdom value and the spiritual health it unleashes in our church.

Today more than 85 percent of our church's adults are in some form of small group. They're happy with their experience, and they tell friends about their group.

If we had stayed with our old system, we could have forced perhaps half the people, at most, to be involved out of a sense of duty, but we would have created a guilt-based system. We would have lost a lot of our passion as well. We would have been banging yesterday's drum and no one would have been listening, comparatively speaking.

If you make adjustments to fit needs, you build trust capital over the years.

Did we get kickback when we made changes? Of course we did. The strongest resistance was in 1980; it was less in 1990. Our 2004 change rolled out with surprising smoothness. We've learned that if you make adjustments to fit needs, you build trust capital over the years. This trust has become part of our culture at Fellowship.

Adapt When It No Longer Unleashes

In my experience of mentoring leaders from other churches, I've found that most of them are teachers and conceptualizers of ideas. They find it hard to put concepts into disciplines that unleash people into ministry. Frank Tillapaugh, whose book *Unleashing the Church* was an early pioneer of this concept, underscores the idea of how much "people progress in their spiritual lives when they are in front-line ministries." In addition, he said, "Lasting motivation comes from within. And nothing motivates more from within [than] being involved in a front-line ministry to which God has called us."[2]

One of our tests for whether a ministry is operating at peak effectiveness is whether it unleashes people to use the gifts they've received from the Holy Spirit. In Chapter Eleven, I described my failing grade at equipping our people to evangelize. I came to the realization after training more than a thousand people in how to share their faith in one-on-one situations. People at Fellowship clearly loved this training—they came wanting to be equipped—but for some reason they didn't follow through afterward and evangelize, even after being equipped to do so. Evangelism was one of our stated values, but sadly, we were still not doing it on a broad scale congregationally. Why?

I began praying: "What do we do?" We purposed not to go for a quick fix by finding and cloning a plug-and-play program. We kept working through our ideals until we could genuinely solve the value issue with a new structure that would unleash it.

> Evangelism was one of our stated values, but sadly, we were still not doing it on a broad scale congregationally. Why?

In our search, we asked ourselves, "What do our people do well?" as it relates to evangelism. We decided that many are excellent connectors who like to bring their friends to church events. We acknowledged the reality that not all people are evangelists, but many have relational gifts.

We asked the same question of our up-front leadership: "What do we do well?" We decided that what Tim Lundy and I do best is teach and evangelize. (Tim and I are both on the teaching-pastor team. He is the new directional leader for the church, and I am the most recent directional leader.) But because we are pastors at church, we don't have nearly the connections with unbelievers and seekers as our church members do. So we put those two strengths together and created an outreach called Explore (see Chapter Eleven). In it, we get to teach and offer the gospel, which we do well; and many of our people partner with us by bringing their friends, which fits their relational gifting well. We still have a number of people in our church who are both gifted and trained to do personal evangelism and who do it effectively. Rather, our adjustment simply recognizes the reality of those whose primary gifts lay elsewhere but still need to find a place to participate in evangelism and be affirmed in it.

We made the courageous adjustment of creating a culture that embraced all these realities together.

To compare our decision to the era of Jesus' ministry, most people are like Andrew, the disciple who went and brought a friend to hear Jesus (John 1:40–41). Or they're like the woman at the well who found her friends and invited them to "come, see a man who told me all the things that I have done" (John 4:29). They're better as connectors than as closers.

When we explained the adaptation, our people were noticeably relieved. Various ones said, "Ah, thank you. I'll gladly join with you in that." Instead of forcing them to do something they felt inadequate for, we liberated them.

The result became a culture of empowerment. We allowed people to be who they really are. We found a way to blend together two truths: "I recognize you're not an evangelist" and "but all of us still need to do evangelism." For us it's the best possible combination: you find seekers, I'll share the faith with them, and you do the follow up.

Our people saw that we were working hard to embody our values while protecting them in ways that are Spirit-led. By making a courageous adjustment, we unleashed our value of evangelism at a new level. We were willing to make the changes necessary to get there. More people than ever are now willing to partner with us in evangelism because our new model works from where they are the

> By making a courageous adjustment, we unleashed our value of evangelism at a new level.

strongest. Today we're not just safeguarding the value of evangelism; we're unleashing it.

Model Adaptation
So It Becomes Part *of* Your Culture

We are currently transitioning our leadership team at Fellowship by adding a number of new, younger directional leaders, including Tim. This major transition is intended to safeguard and enhance our totem known as relevance. Our goal is to periodically bring on new leadership in a way that keeps our church pointed at the thirty-something generation. This way we stay young enough for the upcoming generation and old enough for the present generation. We are making these courageous adjustments so as to protect our relevance, even though such adjustments bring a certain risk with them.

One of Fellowship's strengths is the unity and continuity we've experienced. We've had the same team of three primary teaching pastors, including myself as directional leader, for the last twenty-five years. Such unusual continuity has afforded tremendous stability. The downside is that we are all of the same age and generation, and growing older every year.

This reality hit us hard five years ago when a fourth teaching pastor briefly joined us on staff before going out to help lead a new church. He was much younger than the three of us. During his short time on our Little Rock staff, we were amazed at how many affirmations we heard from younger members of our congregation about how his life stage felt more relevant to them. His sermon illustrations spoke to parents like him who had little ones in diapers. He listened to different music. He spent his young-adult years knowing about "Friends," whereas we grew up watching "Father Knows Best." (Even admitting the fact makes me feel old!)

We probed further and found a whole new generation at Fellowship who were feeling a loss because they didn't have someone they could identify with. Our value is to target the thirty-year-old as our primary audience. We realized that it was impossible for our three main teaching pastors to maintain the target, given an aging issue that won't stop. So we decided to intentionally begin a downward shift in the age of our elder board and our pastoral leadership. This would require creative and courageous thinking.

Our solution addressed three levels. First we began to recruit staff who are considerably younger than what we had been comfortable with. We acknowledged that the natural tendency is to hire people in our generation, and we covenanted to push ourselves away from this inclination.

Second, we realized that we needed younger elders. We decided to create a new pre-elder training designed to identify and develop younger leaders for the church. This would give us a sense of those who could be elders in the future while getting them involved now. Interestingly, as we implemented this plan we were surprised at their maturity, and in a matter of a few years we began bringing on a number of them as new elders. We also moved some of our elders to emeritus status, with their agreement, realizing we couldn't have people stay on the board forever. Today a growing number of our elder board are in their thirties, offering to our church and to us older elders a much-needed perspective and balance for the future.

Our third transition involved the teaching pastors themselves. We created a five-year plan that would reposition the original teaching pastors into various ministries and gradually move us away from the Sunday pulpit. Bill Wellons went first, preaching less and less, while Tim Lundy, our thirty-seven-year-old directional leader, took his place as Fellowship's primary pulpiteer.

I'll be next. As this book goes to press, we are in the process of finding an additional younger teaching pastor who can rotate onto our preaching team while I transition into other ministries in our church as pastor at large.

I've already transitioned my hat as directional leader to Tim. This means, in part, he now does up to half the preaching while my pulpit time, along with Bill Parkinson's, is reduced.

The congregation's response to all of this has been both gracious and understanding. Much of it is because of the trust capital the three of us have established here over twenty-five years.

In no way do Bill Wellons, Bill Parkinson, and I feel demoted or pushed aside. I get to preach and teach around the country. I'm not working less either. Instead, I have the opportunity to be a pioneer in new arenas of ministry. In the process, I'm also pioneering what can be done by a church that wants to stay relevant to its culture.

I could have stayed on as directional leader for many more years, and the church would have grown older in many ways with me. Instead, I can now invest myself more with writing, consulting, and developing resources for other churches to use, such as my Men's Fraternity film series (www.mensfraternitycom), all with the best of my creative ideas, while turning over the church's directional leadership to someone younger. The shift started as I asked myself, "How long will you be relevant to the *whole* church?" Instead of feeling threatened, I believe I'm taking on a greater challenge: multiplying myself through others.

To maintain a vibrant multigenerational church, multiplication must be present at every level, including the top-level leadership. This leads to a positive, stable succession—the hardest kind to accomplish, according to management expert Peter Drucker. It starts with my commitment for the church to do well after I'm no longer at the helm. Second, if I'm to transition the church to the leadership of someone else, I've got to get out of the way. To do so also means I must develop a "second half" ministry life for myself, which I'm currently doing.

Fellowship Bible Church is far bigger than me. I may have helped build it, loving every minute, but now I've got to give it away, anointing and endorsing someone else to run with it. I believe God will use our new future leaders to take the church to a greater level of success because I have held to and modeled our value of relevance.

At Fellowship, our forms are perpetually shifting in order to release our core values at their maximum level.

SOMETIMES CHANGE IS ESSENTIAL

When I became a Christian during college, I attended a church that was surprisingly cutting-edge for the 1960s. The pastor used life-based, highly relevant illustrations as he applied God's Word to my world of that day. The choir rocked, swayed, and sounded like today's Brooklyn Tabernacle choir; the main instruments were acoustic guitars and a bass fiddle, rather than an organ. The worship leader looked and dressed like Doc Severinsen, music director of the old "Tonight Show" with Johnny Carson.

The church, adjacent to a college campus, attracted thousands of college students. It was a seedbed in certain ways for many of the ideas that later became Fellowship Bible Church. Its influence on me and others has been profound and long-lasting.

Recently I went to advise a pastoral search committee there, and I discovered that the congregation today is only a ghost of what it once was. In the 1980s and 1990s, when other churches began shifting to small groups, worship choruses, live drama, and new technology, this church balked, as did its pastor. Rather than continue to make adjustments (after all, he himself had once been a pacesetter), he kept his same approach. In doing so, he sacrificed the very value that he had once drawn thousands with: relevance.

What worked so well and inspired so many in the 1960s and 1970s became locked into a style that did not work in the 1980s and 1990s. The model that once impressed me as being relevant and cutting edge became a victim of age. As the church balked at making courageous adjustments, many members transitioned elsewhere. Students from the nearby college fell away too.

The point is this: values should never be confused with form. It's easy to do so, but it's deadly when it happens. Kingdom values must stay partnered with expressions and forms that are current with and fit for the times. That's the job of leadership. As leaders, we must be willing to make whatever courageous adjustments are necessary, to let our values—God's values—succeed and thrive within our congregations. When we do, we safeguard not just these values but also our church's future.

> Values should never be confused with form.

Advancing the Culture

A German tourist in the United States, unfamiliar with American sports, is enjoying one of our public parks. As he sits, he watches several young people throwing a Frisbee back and forth.

One of them comes his way to get a drink from the water fountain, so he asks her a question. "I've been watching you for the last fifteen minutes. May I trouble you to tell me: Which one of you is winning?"

Americans, if known for nothing else, are recognized as people who value competition. But the observer, in looking for a rivalry, missed the point of how Frisbee is played.

In today's church we often look for the wrong things and miss the point. We try to figure out who's winning rather than search out the more substantive questions of "What's really going on here?" and "How did this church develop to this particular stage?" and "What are the totems that hold this church together?"

Suppose the German tourist left the Frisbee game and went to church but made a similar miss-the-point observation. He might notice excitement about worship and conclude that it's because of the new multimedia projector. He might observe a thriving singles ministry and attribute its success to the church's new cappuccino bar. He might look at the youth retreat and decide it works well because they go to a rock-climbing wall.

His mistake is to focus on successful programs or successful tools—externals such as a rock climbing wall—rather than focusing on how God is working in the lives of the youth sponsors manning the wall, being equipped to serve, and developing into a caring team. He'd be wrong to think the rock-climbing wall produced the effect of ministry, rather than vice versa.

• • • • •

This final part shows what happens when churches do "get it," when they shift away from the wrong ideas of how to build a culture (superficial things, plug-in programs, clones of someone else) and instead find an incarnational way to grow a healthy, God-honoring culture.

Irresistible Culture

IN GUIDING THEIR CHILDREN TOWARD MATURITY, good parents generally avoid a rigid, one-approach-fits-all formula. Yet they do follow many progressions: toddlers must learn to walk before they can run, children learn responsibility in stages, and teens are granted later curfews as they prove themselves to be trustworthy.

Similarly, church leaders are wise to tailor whatever they do to lead their congregations through a culture shift, even as they follow this overall progression:

1. Identify and believe God's promises about your church's potential.
2. Model kingdom culture personally.
3. Enlist allies to champion the culture shift.
4. Focus on "what we're becoming."
5. Compare the vision of the future to present reality.
6. Outline a specific, doable pathway.
7. Help it filter through the church, and learn from feedback you receive.
8. Stay focused on transformed people, and on those receptive to change.

9. Make heroes of people who best represent the kingdom values.

10. Celebrate every success, and give God the glory.

How many of these steps have you taken? How well are they working?

A healthy culture allows a church to grow naturally, like an orchard. An unhealthy culture usually has someone pulling at it, pushing it, or mandating that it function in certain ways. If you can develop the right culture, stuff grows on its own and genuine innovation thrives.

As you awaken to the importance of church culture, you might view your own church's culture as an invisible megaphone. Your culture broadcasts its identity far and wide. It communicates messages even if you don't realize it.

> A healthy culture allows a church to grow naturally. If you can develop the right culture, stuff grows on its own.

As a shepherd and leader, your job is to steward your life and leadership so well that you can create a God-glorifying, delightful culture that will bear much fruit. You can, by God's power and grace, lead your church's culture into a shift that has ripple effects through your community and far beyond. We know you can, because it's happening all around the world.

YOU ARE PART of SOMETHING GLOBAL

Fellowship Bible Church has a global vision, and over the years we've sent representatives of our church to many parts of the world. Some do ministry in established churches, while others help to start new churches. One of the established churches we partner with invited me to visit them, and I was eager to do so.

What I found was a classic example of a church whose leaders are in desperate need of a culture shift. The church had plateaued for some time, but in recent years it experienced a wonderful revitalization. Unfortunately, the elders there attributed the growth to the wrong source and are now in trouble because they're continuing to take an outside-in approach to transitioning their culture.

The culture confusion started shortly after a resident from Fellowship helped train members of the church in lay ministry, with the full blessing of the church's pastor and elder board. The church's leadership even allowed these newly equipped and energized members to start their own hands-on ministries. Soon these new leaders began using their gifts and abilities to connect the church with the community. The results included growth that was especially visible through a new wave of young people coming into the church.

At the same time, the elders were speaking to the church about the possibility of a new facility. Unfortunately, they came to believe that this vision was largely responsible for much of the new growth and that a new facility would bring even more growth. So they led the church into a serious building campaign, completely overlooking what was really behind the new life. They were deep into this building project when I visited, but running short of money. Things were getting desperate. They now wanted their group of active lay leaders to come up with ideas for how to raise more funds for the new facility, not realizing that these people saw no need for a building but only for new ways to do life-on-life ministry.

The established leaders viewed the totem of their church's culture as a brick-and-mortar form: "The new facility will make us more reputable and attractive. It will bring in more people." They obviously felt they were doing something right, and that a new building would release and allow even more ministry. The recent surge of momentum made them feel endorsed, but in actuality the church was growing despite their efforts.

Clearly they were missing the point. This new growth came from a budding new culture, not from the vision of a new building. A serious tension has now developed as the new vibrant lay leaders want additional help and support for their new ministries,

New growth came from a budding new culture, not from the vision of a new building.

but the elders are instead putting all their energy and all available dollars into the building program.

The elders think the right building makes all the difference. In reality, the new surge of life is organic, almost irrelevant to facility issues. Its totems center on equipping and empowering the people of the church, and building the right values into people's lives. When these new lay leaders were asked (I did so), they said to forget about the new building, take the money, and use it instead to hire staff who will help the people of the church establish additional relationships with their community. They want to be part of a new church culture that flows from the energy of their spiritual lives, but instead they feel they're being used to propagate an old paradigm that doesn't work.

It seems clear where God wants to take the church, but the established leaders can't see it as their future. I've encouraged both sides to move toward one another in some much-needed dialogue. Hopefully in time they'll discern the Holy Spirit's leading and find a new sense of unity in a church transformed from the inside out.

Such examples are not limited to overseas venues. I recently attended a church out west that was once perceived as the leading church in the entire state but somehow has now lost its edge in how to grow a life-giving culture. Attendance has steadily declined in the process, with the average age in the pew increasing to the point of being easily twenty years older than the surrounding community. Ministry forms froze as if every year were still 1955.

The church's answer was to build a multimillion-dollar facility in a new location with easy access from the interstate highway. They went into high-risk debt to do so and are still feeling the financial pinch today. But worse than the strangulating debt is how they relocated for the wrong reason. They're wrongly betting on the facility as their culture. It's not.

How to Think, Not What to Think

This final chapter is called "Irresistible Culture." It describes how you know when you're getting there—how your congregation of young spiritual billionaires looks as they gain their inheritance (see Chapter

One) and as they revel in it. It affirms what the environment of your church can be as it comes of age.

The emphasis of *Culture Shift* has been on becoming a life-giving church filled with Spirit-led people who minister from the energy of their life in the Son, who are released and encouraged to pursue what their heavenly Father has called them to do. Leaders in these churches do not foster environments through the misplaced idea that imported programs, bigger facilities, longer preaching, or cloned forms from somewhere else make a church healthy.

Instead, the lifestyles of spiritually energized people *are* the convincing point in a culturally healthy congregation. They also realize that true revival transforms society as well as souls.

This book has been about *how* to think, not *what* to think. It's been about a concept, not a program. It was designed to offer a life-long heartbeat rather than a quick, short-term energy boost.

Culture Shift has affirmed that the day of plug-and-play ministry is over. If you focus on outward forms like Lincoln Logs, you'll build an organization that wears you down. Leaders today need to build a culture, because a church is an organism more than it is an organization. As you nurture the formation of a culture through the power of the Spirit, the organisms grow. You can build a bad culture and bacteria will grow, but a good culture will produce fruit.

> True revival transforms society as well as souls. The lifestyles of spiritually energized people are the convincing point.

This book asks how to restore the eye of the tiger in you, so that you have a renewed heart. It's about developing a congregation that's running to win more than tagging along with the rest of the pack. It speaks to good people who are weary of always trying to push and pull ministry, concerned it might die from inaction without them.

The life of a leader is not to be the way many very-busy-but-aimless churches function, as Paul reminds us: "Do you not know that in a race all the runners run, but only one gets the prize? Run in such a way as to get the prize. Everyone who competes in the games goes into strict training. They do it to get a crown that will not last; but we do it to get a crown that will last forever" (1 Corinthians 9:24–25, NIV). We need to know where we're going, and to have a desire to succeed at doing so.

How Does It Feel When You're Getting Close?

When either of us goes shopping with our wife, we decide within seconds of walking into a store, "This is a classy place" or "This feels cheap." You just know. Culture has a way of communicating itself, typically in little ways everywhere. How people smile or greet you, the cleanliness, the quality, the décor all send signals about what's really going on here. A church—whether it's gathering in a worship facility, in a home, or in the community—sends the same signals. Anyone can discern within seconds of contact that "This is a healthy place" or "Something's not right here." It may take you weeks to figure out why, but the signs are everywhere.

In a church living out its inheritance, people say things like, "The minute I walked in, I knew God was here." It's the energy, how people smile, and all the unspoken but unmistakable gestures that say hope, love, nurture, vision, and direction.

Years ago, a man at Fellowship Bible Church was always talking about how great the church is. Today he speaks primarily about the ministry God put him into. The difference is a them-and-us comparison. Today, he's not describing something out there; it's coming out of his life.

> In a church living out its inheritance, people say, "The minute I walked in, I knew God was here."

The measurement of a culturally solid church is that with all its facets, from children's ministry to adult Bible studies and corporate worship, one simple factor shows you if you're there: How are people talking about it afterward? Are they talking out of

Indeed

their gut on Wednesday morning after the men's meeting? Are youths coming back from the retreat talking to their parents about what they learned about their relationship with God? Are people telling friends about something that happened in their small groups? The conversation cannot be limited to what they receive, or the impact of the church in their lives; more personally, it also needs to address the ministry *they're* doing or thinking about doing.

> If people regularly use the language of life change, you know the church is advancing a healthy culture.

Yes, people talk too about your latest gimmick, something zany the preacher or worship leader or youth pastor did to drive home a point. They also talk about the big concerts you sponsor, the art exhibit you create, or any other larger-than-life experiences you offer. They are fun to tell others about, but look as well for talk about how God used the principle of the sermon to change their life. Maybe someone gave up a certain idol, or learned how to forgive a rebellious child, or understood faith for the first time. If people use the language of life change after your meetings end, and if they do so enthusiastically and repeatedly, you know the church is advancing a healthy culture.

CHURCH *of* DREAM RELEASERS

I was born in Hawaii and minister there at New Hope now, but my family didn't always live there. In my book *The Dream Releasers*,[1] I tell the story of when I was a junior high school student in Japan and paid 100 yen to release a finch. I went to the crest of a mountain and watched it hop out of the cage and soar over the edge of the mountain, flying effortlessly over the open ravine. The joy I felt for that bird put a big smile on my face and in my heart as well. The feeling I had was worth a million yen.

In the same way, if God can find a church with dream releasers then how many young dreamers will God send to it? Like the story of my wife and baby daughter in Chapter Two, God is looking for nurseries to care for his children. If you make good nurseries, he will fill them.

Were you ever a resident in one of those nurseries? Did God ever send you to someone who believed in you more than you did yourself (1 Thessalonians 3:2), who accepted you (Romans 15:7), who always looked for the best in you (1 Corinthians 13:7, The Message), who saw Christ being formed in you (Galatians 4:19), and who affirmed that God is at work in you (Philippians 1:6)?

For me, it was a Bible college teacher. I was saved through a rock-and-roll background. I took the paperback *New Testament* that Campus Crusade had given me, and I went to Bible school. In my second class, on Bible history, the teacher was Grace Flint. She affirmed me, saying, "God's going to use you. The kingdom of God awaits you." So I took every class that woman taught.

> God gives his best in potential form, and the culture you set determines whether it will grow, stagnate, or die.

A bar of steel is worth about $32 if you convert it into sixteen-penny nails. Its value goes up to $200 if you make it into needles, to $3,500 if it becomes Ginsu knives, and to $250,000 if converted into Swiss watch springs. It's the same bar, but everything depends on what potential you see in it.

The heart of this book has affirmed that you, as a leader in the church, have the privilege of setting the culture for your congregation. Every church has extremely great potential. You as a leader will cause it to fly or die, release or decease, be prophetic or be pathetic. God gives his best in potential form, and the culture you set determines whether it will grow, stagnate, or die.

Every four years, as the United States votes on a new president, sometimes the incumbent wins and sometimes he loses. Then afterward everyone tries to figure out why. Bill Clinton summarized his upset of George Herbert Walker Bush with these four simple words: "It's the economy, stupid."

We're convinced that four similar words explain the health difference between churches: "It's the culture, stupid." It's not the building, or the program, or the latest gimmick, or even the size of the crowd. Neither bigness nor smallness is a guarantee of health. Even innovation just for innovation's sake is dead.

The chapter opened with a church where the buzz was, "Why are we building this building?" The leaders were out of touch, and people were feeling used. Instead, the growth tip was in meeting a God who can change them, in hanging around people in the church whom God has already changed, and in experiencing the release of seeing God work through "my" life to touch others.

Life-giving, God-encountering churches are attractive, inviting, and irresistible; they bring a sense of rest as well as direction. Like traveling in the right current of a stream, you can relax. There's a rest present, but also a direction as you move, that takes you across city, state, country, and beyond.

The experience is similar to what happened in Jesus' day on the road to Emmaus. The disciples said their hearts were "burning within us" (Luke 24:32) because they encountered Jesus along the way. This is what culture-rich churches feel like to people who encounter them: people's hearts start burning even before they recognize why. They feel the movement that the culture is exuding long before they understand what it's really about. They're still talking about it even after Jesus disappears.

WHEN YOU'RE THERE, YOU'LL KNOW

To us nothing is better than a church that is excited about how God is working through it. What better way to feel about your church than for this statement to be true: "I'm part of a leading influence in my community. It gives me great joy to see how God is using our church to shape the culture even beyond our church and to make our community a better place, spiritually and in every other way."

When that happens we find ourselves linked back to the early days of the gospel, when outsiders observed, "These people who have been turning the world upside down have come here also" (Acts 17:6, NRSV).

In culture-rich churches people's hearts start burning even before they recognize why.

During the Welsh revival of 1904, many taverns went bankrupt because drunkenness was immediately cut in half. Crime was so diminished that judges ran out of cases. Even the police became unemployed in many districts.[2] The revival had a ripple effect in other towns, the entire country, and across the world.[3] The story is told of a tourist to Wales during this era, traveling by train, who said to the conductor, "Where's the revival? Where's a church with people having these unique encounters with God?" The conductor replied, "Just start walking, and you'll know."

When your church advances a healthy culture and it becomes reality, the result is a drawing effect that people will come out of the woodwork to experience. And it will be contagious to everyone who encounters it.

The culture shift begins by believing in the potential of the people God has already given you, and then releasing the right culture through them.

The culture shift begins by believing in the potential of the people God has already given you, and then releasing the right culture through them. As the culture grows and matures, it transforms your church from the inside out. In the end, people all over town will begin to say, along with the train conductor a century ago, "Is something different about that church? Simply come across a few of its people, and you'll know."

And when that happens, you will say, "Glory to God!"

If the culture changes, everything else changes, including the future.

Notes

Foreword

1. McManus, Erwin Raphael. *An Unstoppable Force: Daring to Become the Church God Had in Mind*. Loveland, Colo.: Group Publishing, 2001. See especially pp. 96–111.
2. McManus, 2001, p. 111.

Chapter One

1. Hofstede, G. *Culture and Organizations, Software of the Mind: Intercultural Cooperation and Its Importance for Survival*. New York: McGraw-Hill, 1996.

Chapter Two

1. Warren, R. *The Purpose-Driven Life: What on Earth Am I Here for?* Grand Rapids, Mich.: Zondervan, 2002, p. 17.
2. Slaughter, M., with Bird, W. *UnLearning Church: Transforming Spiritual Leadership for the Emerging Church*. Loveland, Colo.: Group, 2002, p. 24.

Chapter Three

1. George, C., with Bird, W. *Nine Keys to Effective Small-Group Leadership*. Mansfield, Pa.: Kingdom, 1997, p. 46; see also p. 68.

2. Cordeiro, W. *Attitudes That Attract Success.* Ventura, Calif.: Gospel Light/Regal, 2001.

3. Collins, J. *Good to Great.* New York: HarperCollins, 2001. See also Collins, C. "Good to Great's Leadership Model Looks Familiar to Christians." *Christianity Today.* 2003. Accessed Jan. 24, 2005. (www.christianitytoday.com/ct/2003/110/51.0.html)

4. Collins (2001), p. 164.

5. Collins (2001), p. 15.

CHAPTER FIVE

1. Barna, G. *The Power of Vision.* Ventura, Calif.: Gospel Light/Regal, 1992, p. 28.

CHAPTER SIX

1. Ogden, G. *Transforming Discipleship: Making Disciples a Few at a Time.* Downers Grove, Ill.: InterVarsity Press, 2003, p. 63.

CHAPTER SEVEN

1. See www.enewhope.org, where you'll find a link for Doing Church as a Team (or "conferences").

2. Cordeiro, W. *Doing Church as a Team* (2nd ed.). Ventura, Calif.: Gospel Light/Regal, 2001.

CHAPTER ELEVEN

1. For the history of Fellowship Bible Church, see www.fbclr.org/about/fbc story.shtml.

2. Lewis, R., with Wilkins, R. *The Church of Irresistible Influence.* Grand Rapids, Mich.: Zondervan, 2001; see esp. pp. 64–67.

3. Here are two of the most recent examples: Mallory, S. *The Equipping Church: Serving Together to Transform Lives.* Grand Rapids, Mich.: Zondervan, 2001; and Mallory, S., and Smith, B. *The Equipping Church Guidebook.* Grand Rapids, Mich.: Zondervan, 2001.

4. Warren, R. *The Purpose-Driven Life.* Grand Rapids, Mich.: Zondervan, 2002, p. 251.

5. Barna, G. *Evangelism That Works: How to Reach Changing Generations with the Unchanging Gospel.* Ventura, Calif.: Gospel Light/Regal, 1995.

6. Sermon by Rick Warren, "Our Global P.E.A.C.E. Plan: You Can Change Your World" (Part One), preached Nov. 1–2, 2003. (www.pastors.com); see also Wooding, D. "Kay Warren Talks About Her 'Damascus Call' to Help People with HIV/AIDS Around the World." Accessed Jan. 24, 2005. (www.pastors.com/article.asp?ArtID=6815)

CHAPTER THIRTEEN

1. Lewis, R., with Wilkins, R. *The Church of Irresistible Influence.* Grand Rapids, Mich.: Zondervan, 2001, esp. pp. 193–194.

2. MacDonald, G. *Restoring Your Spiritual Passion.* Nashville, Tenn.: Thomas Nelson, 1986.

CHAPTER FOURTEEN

1. Getz, G. A. *Building Up One Another.* Colorado Springs, Colo.: David C. Cook, 1976; Getz, G. A. *Sharpening the Focus of the Church.* Chicago: Moody, 1976.

2. Tillapaugh, F. *Unleashing the Church: Getting People out of the Fortress and into Ministry.* Ventura, Calif.: Gospel Light/Regal, 1982, pp. 129, 131.

CHAPTER FIFTEEN

1. Cordeiro, W. *The Dream Releasers: How to Help Others Realize Their Dreams While Achieving Your Own.* Ventura, Calif.: Gospel Light/Regal, 2002.

2. Orr, J. E. *The Flaming Tongue: Evangelical Awakenings, 1900.* Chicago: Moody, 1975.

3. Towns, E., and Porter, D. *The Ten Greatest Revivals Ever.* Ventura, Calif.: Gospel Light/Regal, 2000.

Appendix One
Involvement and Satisfaction Survey

(Adapted from Fellowship Bible Church, Little Rock, Arkansas; www.fbclr.org)

Instructions: Thank you for taking the time to offer your candid responses to these questions. Please:

1. Read each statement or question carefully.
2. Circle, check, or enter your candid response to each question.
3. Provide no response if the statement or question doesn't apply.

When finished, please fold, place in the envelope you received, seal, and return to your small group leader, ministry leader, usher/greeter, or place in the offering plate. Thanks again for your participation.

1. Your age and gender?

   Age: 20 or under   21–35   36–50   51–65   66 or older
   Gender: _____ M   _____ F

2. How long have you attended the church?

   1–2 yrs.   3–5 yrs.   6–8 yrs.   9–11 yrs.   12 yrs. or more

3. Marital status?

   Married   Divorced   Separated   Single

4. How satisfied are you with the strength of your marriage?

   (very dissatisfied)   1   2   3   4   5   (very satisfied)

5. How satisfied are you with the condition of your family?

   (very dissatisfied)   1   2   3   4   5   (very satisfied)

6. If you have children, how many and what are their ages?
   (If none, skip to question 11)

   1   2   3   4   5   6   more   (circle one)

   Ages   ____   ____   ____   ____   ____   ____

7. If you have children, are they actively involved in our
   children's ministry?

   Yes   No   (If *no*, please skip to question 9)

8. How satisfied are you with your experience with our
   children's ministry?

   (very dissatisfied)   1   2   3   4   5   (very satisfied)

9. If you have junior or senior high school students, are they
   actively involved in our student ministries?

   Yes   No   (If *no*, please skip to question 11)

10. How satisfied are you with your experience with our student
    ministries?

    (very dissatisfied)   1   2   3   4   5   (very satisfied)

11. Which worship service do you normally attend, and how
    often?

    _____ (example: Sunday 8:00 A.M.)

Frequency of attendance: 3–4 times/mo.

1–2 times/mo.   5–10 times/yr.   1–4 times/yr.

12. How satisfied are you overall with your personal weekend worship experience?

(very dissatisfied)   1   2   3   4   5   (very satisfied)

13. How satisfied are you with the personal impact of weekend preaching on your life?

(very dissatisfied)   1   2   3   4   5   (very satisfied)

14. How satisfied are you with the personal impact of our present weekend worship style?

(very dissatisfied)   1   2   3   4   5   (very satisfied)

15. Which of these newcomer classes have you completed?

_____ Discovery 1   _____ Discovery 2

16. If you have experienced Discovery class in the past three years, how satisfied were you with it?

(very dissatisfied)   1   2   3   4   5   (very satisfied)

17. Are you actively involved in a Community Group?

Yes   No   (If *no*, please skip to question 19)

18. How satisfied are you with your present Community Group experience?

(very dissatisfied)   1   2   3   4   5   (very satisfied)

19. Are you actively serving in any ministry in or through our church?

Yes   No   (If *no*, please skip to question 21)

20. How satisfied are you with your present serving experience at our church?

(very dissatisfied)   1   2   3   4   5   (very satisfied)

21. Are you actively involved in one of Fellowship's men's or women's classes?

    Yes   No   (If *no*, please skip to question 23)

22. How satisfied are you with your experience in your present men's or women's class?

    (very dissatisfied)   1   2   3   4   5   (very satisfied)

23. How often do you spend devotional time reading your Bible?

    Almost daily   a few times a week   a few times a month
    a few times a year

24. How satisfied are you with your experience when you spend time in your Bible?

    (very dissatisfied)   1   2   3   4   5   (very satisfied)

25. How often do you spend time in prayer?

    Almost daily   a few times a week   a few times a month
    a few times a year

26. How satisfied are you with your experience when you spend time in prayer?

    (very dissatisfied)   1   2   3   4   5   (very satisfied)

27. How consistent are your daily choices with biblical standards of morality?

    (very inconsistent)   1   2   3   4   5   (very consistent)

28. How satisfied are you with your spiritual growth over this past year?

    (very dissatisfied)   1   2   3   4   5   (very satisfied)

29. How many people have you taken through One-to-One this year?

    None   1   2   3   4 or more

30. How many people have you shared the gospel with in some form this year?

    None   1   2   3   4 or more

31. How many people have accepted Jesus personally with you this year?

    None   1   2   3   4 or more

32. How many Equipping Center classes have you taken in total at our church?

    None   1   2   3   4 or more   (If none, please skip to question 34)

33. How satisfied were you with your most recent Equipping Center class experience?

    (very dissatisfied)   1   2   3   4   5   (very satisfied)

34. Roughly, what percentage of your total income do you give to this church on an annual basis?

    0%   1–3%   4–6%   7–9%   10% or more

35. How would you describe the pattern of your giving to our church?

    Weekly   monthly   twice monthly   quarterly   semiannually   annually

36. How many days in the last twelve months did you invest at least part of the day in personal community service?

    None   1–3 days   4–7 days   8–10 days   11 or more days

37. How would you express your level of satisfaction with your overall experience at our church?

    (very dissatisfied)   1   2   3   4   5   (very satisfied)

Appendix Two
Sample Pages from a Life Journal

At New Hope Christian Fellowship O'ahu (www.enewhope.org), a majority of the church is involved with making daily "Life Journal" entries as they read and apply the Bible. The journals have a generic layout that makes them usable by hundreds of other churches as well. A sample entry is presented here.

Life Journals follow a "S.O.A.P." pattern, where users read a passage of **S**cripture and highlight a verse or phrase the Lord impresses on them as a personal word to be applied. Next they make an **o**bservation about it, write a paragraph of **a**pplication to their life, and then finish by writing a **p**rayer, asking God for strength and wisdom to live according to what they've just experienced. Users also create a contents page, designed to help them when they look back later, wanting to recall their learnings and the attitude of heart with which they received the lesson.

The goal is to see a change taking place, a fertility in someone's heart like a tree growing and bearing fruit. It's a daily self-feeding program consistent with the relentless pursuing of God, inspired by this promise: "You will seek me and find me when you search for me with all your heart" (Jeremiah 29:13).

Daily Pages, Sample Entry

DATE	TITLE	PAGE
4/23	"Marching Orders" (topic: prayer)	2

Scripture

"What I tell you in the darkness, speak in the light; and what you hear whispered in your ear, proclaim upon the housetops" (Matthew 10:27).

Observation

If I am not hearing God in the darkness, what will I speak in the light? If I am not hearing him whisper in my ear, what will I proclaim on the housetops?

Application

*What a great word! This Scripture reminds me to not only talk to God in prayer, but equally important to **hear** him in prayer!*

Prayer

"Dear Jesus, help me to hear you today! I want to be still that I may hear your marching orders for my day, for my week, for my life. Speak Lord! Your servant is listening."

Bibliography

Books *by* ROBERT LEWIS

Authentic Manhood—Winning at Work and Home (sixteen-session LifeWay DVD series)

The Church of Irresistible Influence

The Great Adventure (twenty-session LifeWay DVD series)

The Quest for Authentic Manhood (twenty-four-session LifeWay DVD series)

Raising a Modern-Day Knight

Real Family Values

Rocking the Roles: Building a Win-Win Marriage

Books *by* WAYNE CORDEIRO

Attitudes That Attract Success

Doing Church as a Team

The Dream Releasers

Gems Along the Way

Indispensable Life Lessons

Living Life Above the Rubble

Rising Above: Living a Life of Excellence No Matter What Life Throws You

BOOKS *with* WARREN BIRD *as* COLLABORATIVE AUTHOR

The Coming Church Revolution

The Comprehensive Guide to Cassette Ministry

The Emotionally Healthy Church: A Strategy for Discipleship That Actually Changes Lives

How to Break Growth Barriers

Into the Future: Turning Today's Church Trends into Tomorrow's Opportunities

Lost in America: How Your Church Can Impact the World Next Door

Nine Keys to Effective Small-Group Leadership: How Lay Leaders Can Establish Healthy Cells, Classes, and Teams

On-Purpose Leadership: Multiplying Your Ministry by Becoming a Leader of Leaders

Prepare Your Church for the Future

Real Followers: Beyond Virtual Christianity

Starting a New Church: How to Plant a High-Impact Congregation

Twelve Emerging Churches: Using Imagination to Identify Your Church's Unique Signature

UnLearning Church: Transforming Spiritual Leadership for the Emerging Church

BOOKS *by* ERWIN RAPHAEL MCMANUS
(FOREWORD)

The Barbarian Way: Unleash the Untamed Faith Within

The Church in Emerging Culture: Five Perspectives (contributing author)

Seizing Your Divine Moment: Dare to Live a Life of Adventure

Unstoppable Force: Daring to Become the Church God Had in Mind

Uprising: A Revolution of the Soul

Acknowledgments

Culture Shift has been a team effort. It would not have been possible without the enthusiastic support of Leadership Network and their mission to connect innovators to multiply. Special thanks goes to Bob Buford, visionary social entrepreneur and personal friend to all three authors; Tom Wilson, nurturing friend and CEO; Dave Travis, a culture-savvy advisor; Carol Childress, the culture maven who got the book started; and Greg Ligon, who affirmed us at each step. Also many thanks to Gary Dungan and Julia Burk for their proofreading expertise.

Robert Lewis especially thanks Tracy Noble and Jeannie Steger for administrative help, and also various staff who have made editorial suggestions, among them Tim Lundy and Steve Snider.

Wayne Cordeiro likewise acknowledges the administrative help of the gracious team at New Hope Fellowship and the life input of Elwin Ahu, Mark Olmos, and Tim Savage.

Warren Bird especially thanks his wife, Michelle Bird, and her prayer partner, Marianna Avarali, who interceded weekly from this book's start to its finish.

Erwin Raphael McManus, who wrote the Foreword, brainstormed with us at a crucial turning point. Mike Slaughter gave us important insight on the concept of unlearning. Elmer Towns, longtime friend of all three authors, offered us wise counsel and assistance.

Sheryl Fullerton, Naomi Lucks, Andrea Flint, and Thomas Finnegan, all associated with Jossey-Bass, showed tremendous editorial talent, grace, flexibility, and insight.

We owe a special debt of thanks to each person who read and offered helpful comments on drafts of the book: Pat Colgan, Michael Cox, Dan Cupp, Bill Easum, Mark Edwards, Kep James, John Jung, Jeff Lind, Dawn O'Brien, Warren Schuh, John Soper, Pat Springle, Tim Volkman, and Mary Waialeale.

About the Authors

Robert Lewis is pastor at large of Fellowship Bible Church (www.fbclr.org), a nondenominational church in Little Rock, Arkansas, with worship attendance of more than six thousand. The church was formed in 1977 and he has been on staff since 1980, serving as directional leader (equivalent of senior pastor) for most of those years. The church has received national acclaim for its role as a model of effective community transformation, powerfully influencing the world around it in strategic, life-giving ways.

Lewis, who was born and raised in Louisiana, has authored a number of books, among them *Raising a Modern-Day Knight, Rocking the Roles: Building a Win-Win Marriage, Real Family Values,* and *The Church of Irresistible Influence.* He is also a contributing author to *Building Strong Families,* edited by Dennis Rainey; and *Faith Factor in Fatherhood,* edited by Don Eberly. He has been featured on radio programs such as "FamilyLife Today" and "Focus on the Family," and in a number of magazines, including *Leadership, Real Man,* and *Stand Firm.*

He also serves as chairman of the board of Fellowship Associates (www.fellowshipassociates.com), a church consulting and leadership training organization responsible for planting twenty-seven new churches to date.

Lewis is also passionate about helping men discover the biblical principles of authentic manhood. In 1990 he founded Men's Fraternity (www.mensfraternity.com); today this significant ministry is reaching men worldwide in churches, on college campuses, in corporate boardrooms, and in prison cellblocks via audio and video. Lewis's teachings are featured in three Men's Fraternity DVD series published by LifeWay: *The Quest for Authentic Manhood* (twenty-four sessions), *Authentic Manhood—Winning at Work and Home* (sixteen sessions), and *The Great Adventure* (twenty sessions). In 2001, he was named Pastor of the Year by the National Coalition of Men's Ministry, headed by Patrick Morley.

Lewis graduated from the University of Arkansas and obtained an M.A. in New Testament Greek and the M.Div. degree, both from Western Seminary, Portland, Oregon. He received the doctor of ministry degree from Talbot Theological Seminary, La Mirada, California.

He and his wife, Sherard, have four children.

Wayne Cordeiro is senior pastor of New Hope Christian Fellowship O'ahu (www.enewhope.org), a Foursquare church with worship attendance of more than ten thousand in Honolulu, Hawaii, making it one of the twenty largest-attendance churches in the United States. The church is also noted as one of the fastest-growing churches in the nation. New Hope began in 1995 under Cordeiro's leadership. Almost eight thousand people welcomed Christ into their lives during the church's first six years.

Cordeiro was raised in Hawaii and then lived in Japan for three years. His family then moved to Oregon. After graduation from Bible college, he served with Youth for Christ and as a staff pastor at Faith Center Foursquare Church, before returning to Hawaii to plant a church in Hilo.

Cordeiro has authored seven books: *Doing Church as a Team, Gems Along the Way, Attitudes That Attract Success, Living Life Above the Rubble, Indispensable Life Lessons, The Dream Releasers,* and *Rising Above: Living a Life of Excellence No Matter What Life Throws You.* He is contributing author to several church leadership books and has written articles for various magazines such as *Leadership Journal.* He has also released six music albums to date.

In 1998, he founded Pacific Rim Bible College (www.prbc-hawaii. edu) to train, develop, and support emerging leaders who will plant twenty-first-century churches throughout the world.

Through New Hope International Ministries (www.enhi.org), the church-planting arm of New Hope Christian Fellowship, where he serves as president, Cordeiro has pioneered several innovative conferences that resource existing churches and spur the planting of future churches. It has pioneered fifty-two churches to date in the United States, Hawaii, Philippines, Myanmar, Finland, Japan, Australia, and Kenya.

Cordeiro received a B.A. in pastoral theology from Eugene Bible College in Oregon and did graduate study at the University of Oregon and at Northwest Christian College, Eugene. In 2001 his denomination, the International Church of the Foursquare Gospel, honored him with a doctor of divinity degree.

He and his wife, Anna, have three children.

Warren Bird (www.warrenbird.com), an ordained minister on staff at a church in greater New York City, researches innovative churches and works with their leaders to multiply their evangelistic and disciple-making impact.

A winner of the prestigious Gold Medallion Award for religious book publishing, he has collaboratively authored fourteen books. He has also contributed chapters or sections to five books and authored more than one hundred magazine articles.

He is a graduate of Wheaton College (B.A., M.A.) and Alliance Theological Seminary (M.Div.) and is working toward a Ph.D. in sociology of religion at Fordham University.

He and his wife, Michelle, have two grown children.

Index

215